Library of
Davidson College

WILDLIFE IN TANZANIAN SETTLEMENT POLICY:
THE CASE OF THE SELOUS

by

GORDON MATZKE

FOREIGN AND COMPARATIVE STUDIES/AFRICA SERIES XXVIII

Maxwell School of Citizenship and Public Affairs
Syracuse University
1977

Copyright

1977

by

MAXWELL SCHOOL OF CITIZENSHIP AND PUBLIC AFFAIRS
SYRACUSE UNIVERSITY, SYRACUSE, NEW YORK, U.S.A.

Library of Congress Cataloging in Publication Data
    Matzke, Gordon E.   Tanzanian Settlement Policy.
    Foreign and Comparative Studies: Africa Series; 27
    1. Wildlife conservation--Tanzania--Selous Game Reserve.
    2. Wildlife Management--Tanzania--Selous Game Reserve.
    3. Land Settlement--Tanzania--Selous Game Reserve.
    4. Environmental policy--Selous Game Reserve, Tanzania.
    I. Title. II. Series.
    QL84.6.T3M37   639'.95'096782   77-18175
    ISBN 0-915984-25-3

ABOUT THE AUTHOR . . . .

Gordon Matzke is an Assistant Professor of Geography at Oregon
State University, Corvallis, Oregon. He received his
Ph.D. in Geography from Syracuse University. The
financial support for his field work reported here was
provided by the Foreign Area Fellowship Program of the
Social Science Research Council and the Shell International
Fellowship administered by Syracuse University.

LIST OF TABLES

Tables		Page
1.	Population Changes in Villages Reporting Sleeping Sickness Cases during the 1924-25 Sleeping Sickness Epidemic	37
2.	Records of Major Relocations in the Lives of Some Ngindo People Who Had Formerly Lived in the Selous Game Reserve	49
3.	Elephants Shot for Cultivation Protection in the Southern Province	63
4.	Interviewee Responses to the Former Occurrence of Selected Animals	65
5.	Rank Order of Total Sightings, Numbers, and Average Herd Size	66
6.	Frequency of Encounter with 12 Ungulate Species in the Selous Game Reserve Portion of the Matandu Study Area in Comparison with Reports of Former Inhabitants	68
7.	Computed Densities Per Square Mile for All Species, Seasons and Vegetation Types	79
8.	Seasonal Frequencies of Occurrence of 12 Species in Settled Vs. Unsettled Transect Miles	92
9.	Summary of Data on Natural History And Locational Preference by Species	103

TABLE OF CONTENTS

Page

INTRODUCTION

I. THE SELOUS GAME PRESERVE IN ITS GEOGRAPHICAL AND HISTORICAL PERSPECTIVE

The Location of the Selous
History in the Selous 1

II. THE MATANDU STUDY AREA AND ITS PEOPLE 46

The Selection of the Study Area 46
The Ngindo Inhabitants and the Location of Their Villages 48
The Case Study of Horowe Village 56

III. THE WILDLIFE SCENE 60

The Wildlife Picture in the Past 60
The Methodology of the Wildlife Census 69
Wildlife Patterns in the Study Area 70

IV. THE POTENTIAL FOR CONFLICT BETWEEN WILDLIFE AND PEOPLE 81

The Location of the Wildlife in Relation to the Location of the Villages 81
The Case of Horowe Settlement as a Study in Human-Wildlife Conflict 94
The Mechanisms of Human-Wildlife Conflict ... 98
The Human-Wildlife Interface with Different Animal Strategies for Survival 101
The Human-Wildlife Interface with Different Human Strategies for Survival 107

APPENDIX A - Species List of All Ungulate and Larger Carnivore Species Encountered in the Study Area 112

APPENDIX B - Data Used to Classify Species According to Frequency of Encounter 113

Bibliography 114

LIST OF ILLUSTRATIONS

Figure		Page
1.	Selous Place Names	10
2.	The Rainfall Regime at the Miombo Research Centre.	11
3.	High Density Population Areas	14
4.	Alternative Land Use Proposals for the Selous Game Reserve	15
5.	Traveler's Routes - Selous Game Reserve	19
6.	Peoples of the Selous Circa 1900	20
7.	Nineteenth Century Invasions of the Selous	26
8.	Important Places of the Maji-Maji	30
9.	Position of Forces - December 1916	33
10.	Principal German Force Movements September 1916-June 1917	35
11.	Movements to Closer Settlements 1941-1949	44
12.	Matandu River Study Area	47
13.	Settlement Areas in the Matandu River Study Area	53
14.	Kudu Seasonal Occurrence in Four Vegetation Forms.	72
15.	Hartebeest Seasonal Occurrence in Four Vegetation Forms	72
16.	Duiker Seasonal Occurrence in Four Vegetation Forms	73
17.	Wildebeest Seasonal Occurrence in Four Vegetation Forms	73
18.	Impala Seasonal Occurrence in Four Vegetation Forms	75
19.	Warthog Seasonal Occurrence in Four Vegetation Forms	75
20.	The Spatial Restriction of Wildebeest, Impala and Hartebeest	76

Figure		Page
21.	Elephant Seasonal Occurrence in Four Vegetation Forms	77
22.	Zebra Seasonal Occurrence in Four Vegetation Forms	77
23.	A Comparison of the Degree of Dispersion Shown by Zebra and Elephant	78
24.	Wet Season Distribution of Wildebeest Along Transect Lines with Reference to Short Grass Concentration Areas	82
25.	Wet Season Distribution of Impala Along Transect Lines with Reference to Short Grass Concentration Areas	83
26.	Wet Season Distribution of Zebra Along Transect Lines with Reference to Short Grass Concentration Areas	84
27.	Wet Season Distribution of Hartebeest Along Transect Lines with Reference to Short Grass Concentration Areas	85
28.	Wet Season Distribution of Wildebeest Along Transect Lines with Reference to Settlement Areas	88
29.	Wet Season Distribution of Impala Along Transect Lines with Reference to Settlement Areas . . .	89
30.	Wet Season Distribution of Zebra Along Transect Lines with Reference to Settlement Areas . . .	90
31.	Wet Season Distribution of Hartebeest Along Transect Lines with Reference to Settlement Areas	91
32.	Relationship Between Former Occurrence of Animals and Their Present Affinity for Locations Which Were Never Settled	93
33.	Average Number of Sightings Per Mile Along the Matandu River (all Animals-Late Dry Season) . .	95
34.	Average Number of Sightings Per Mile Along the Matandu River (all Animals-Early Dry Season). .	95

Figure		Page
35.	Average Number of Sightings Per Mile Along the Matandu River (all Animals-Wet Season)	96
36.	Average Number of Sightings Per Mile Along the Matandu River (all Animals-November 29, 1974)	96
37.	Schematic of Ngindo Settlement Patterns	110

INTRODUCTION

Villages are a core feature of Tanzania's economic and political development strategies. Although this village emphasis has policy antecedents stretching back to German occupation, government intervention into village locational processes reached its acme when two-thirds of the populace was moved into Ujamaa Villages between 1972 and 1976. While some have already judged this massive resettlement an "impressive success" (African Update, 1977), the more prudent observer might best await the passage of a decade or two before making any definitive statement on the merits for development of this undertaking.

The settlement policies of Tanzania are discussed regularly in the literature on African economic development (e.g., deSouza & Porter, 1974; Knight & Newman, 1976). This discussion is often based more on the documents churned out by Tanzania's political party than on field research in the villages themselves. This is unfortunate since it is the activities within the villages which in the final analysis will determine the outcome of Tanzania's grand excursion into the uncertainties of resettlement reorganization.

The ecological consequences of the massive resettlement programs are in need of an examination every bit as thorough as that given the political and economic considerations. Since the ecological aspects of resettlement are not discussed in the published party pronouncements, armchair theoreticians have little to inspire their imaginations in this sphere. Nevertheless, even a cursory view of the situation suggests that such a massive reorganization of human settlement activity must have profound consequences for the natural environment.[1]

---

[1] Support for this contention is found in the activities of earlier colonial authorities. Their settlement reorganization activities were often undertaken with the expressed goal of modifying the natural environment in order to control disease vectors such as tsetse fly.

Several authors (Porter, 1976; Kjekshus, 1977) suggest that land use decisions which favor wildlife are detrimental to agriculturalists because of increased depredations from vermin. This contention can only be valid under the circumstances where settlement lends itself to easy animal access because of both proximity and arrangement. Additionally, it requires that the favored species be morphologically and behaviorally predisposed to utilize agricultural crops. Evidence reported in this monograph suggests that many species do not reap advantages from human settlement. By so doing, it illustrates the complexity of the settlement/wildlife equation over both time and space in southeastern Tanzania. It should encourage further discussion of the ecological consequences of Tanzania's settlement policies.

The woodlands of southeastern Tanzania never have been very heavily populated by humans. History and nature have conspired to periodically decimate the residents through wars, famine, and disease. In order to break the grip of one disease, sleeping sickness, an ultimate solution was proposed--the removal of all human inhabitants.

Subsequent to the removal of the scattered villages and the incorporation of large areas into the Selous Game Reserve, observers reported a substantial increase in the numbers of game animals (Nicholson, 1969). Initial investigations (Matzke, 1972) showed that it was unlikely that direct human induced mortality could explain the low wildlife numbers prior to the removal of humans. It was suggested that the human populations had perhaps occupied critical spaces for the maintenance of wildlife and by their occupancy denied these particularly important places to the animals.

This suggestion arose from the examination of archival materials in the light of ecological principles. It was untested and in need of field documentation before its validity could be established. The research discussed in this monograph was designed as an examination of field evidence which would illuminate the role of settlement locations in the total wildlife support system in the particular locality selected for study. In order to do this, it was necessary to segregate the spaces occupied by humans from spaces which had not been occupied. After identifying these "human spaces," it was necessary to determine if there was a differentiation between the resource bases of the human and non-human localities. Last, it was necessary to determine if the wildlife populations were selectively locating on sites which had been occupied by humans in the past, and avoiding equivalent sites which had yet to be abandoned. If this was found to be true, there would be strong support for the hypothesis that human settlement restricts access to areas that are especially important to the maintenance of populations of many species.

The segregation of the total landscape into "human spaces" --places identifiable as having once been settled--and non-human spaces (i.e. never having been settled) was accomplished by the collation of data from three sources. 1) Archival material[1] was searched for maps and reports that would provide a basis for understanding the history of human settlement in the study area. The names of many villages and their approximate locations were sketched and some estimates of previous populations were uncovered, together with the years in which the people were removed. 2) Interviews with former residents now living in the vicinity of the Selous Game Reserve were combined with visits to the study area in order to locate the specific sites where settlements had existed previously. 3) The entire length of the road transect

---

[1] Published and microfilmed material was researched in the Africana collections of Syracuse University, Northwestern University, and the University of Dar es Salaam. A number of historical maps were located in the map collection of Oklahoma State University. The Tanzanian National Archives provided a wealth of information by granting me permission to examine colonial government files including those bearing on game reserves, sleeping sickness control, and provincial administration. (See bibliography for a list of particularly useful files.) In addition, the library, map collection and files of the Miombo Research Centre provided useful information particularly related to the Selous Game Reserve.

system was examined on foot for vegetative and cultural clues that would indicate the former presence of settlement. Each mile was classified as having been settled or not settled. The settled miles were found to be located along the river valleys for the most part.

The survey of the resource base[1] consisted of a classification of vegetation forms along the transect routes, the identification of the more common plant species in 26 sites that were representative of the habitat mix available in the Selous, and an assessment of the general relationship between soil type and edaphic physiography. Surface water availability did not appear to be an important limiting factor on the distribution of most species of animals. The survey of the resource base showed the importance of relief in determining both the soil type and the resultant vegetation formations. The ridge areas contained mostly sandy soils and were covered with either woodland/forest or thicket vegetation forms. The drainage lines, in contrast, contained finer grained soils covered with either scrub or true grasslands. It was these soils that had attracted settlement to the valley locations, and it was the grasslands which made these same locations potentially attractive to many large mammal species. With a clear differentiation of resources between upland and lowland areas established, it remained to be shown that the large mammals responded to that differentiation by showing correspondent locational preferences.

The survey of large mammals was designed to give specific locational information which could be correlated with settlement history, vegetation form, and season of the year. A line transect censusing technique was selected. The transects were laid out and repeatedly counted to ensure that different settlement histories, vegetation forms, and seasons of the year were adequately represented in the data obtained for analysis. The data analysis showed that many species exhibited seasonal spatial

---

[1]This part of the study is reported in detail elsewhere (Matzke, 1975). Only the most important elements are included herein.

shifts which resulted in the great majority of their individuals locating in the grasslands of the river valleys during the rainy season. This resulted in a very nucleated distribution and that nucleation was concentrated on the formerly settled locations.

Interviews were conducted with former inhabitants of the game reserve and their responses suggested that their former village locations lacked many of the species which were found to be very numerous during the transect counts. This was particularly true for the gregarious grazing species. Their responses did not indicate that the more solitary and rare animals of today were absent in the past.

The information gathered on the influence of isolated settlements on the large mammal populations of the Selous Game Reserve is presented in four parts. Chapter One sketches the geographical and historical setting of the Selous Game Reserve. It is shown to be a place of low agricultural potential quite apart from the mainstream of Tanzanian development. Its history is a series of events which have had a debilitating impact on the maintenance of human populations. The ultimate result was the total elimination of humans and their rights of occupance with a 21,000 square mile (55,000 km^2) game reserve replacing them.

Chapter Two narrows the scope of inquiry to the Matandu River Valley in the southeastern part of the game reserve. It is this locality which was selected as a case study since the huge size of the Selous Reserve prohibited close examination. The Matandu Valley was selected because it contained a good representation of the settlement histories and habitats found in the Selous. It had the additional advantage of a serviceable network of tracks. Just downstream, outside of the reserve, there was an active settlement available for comparison with the abandoned settlement areas, and numerous former Selous residents could be interviewed here. Chapter Two includes an introduction to the Ngindo who inhabited it. The settlement pattern of these people is described in general and the particular example of Horowe Village is discussed in detail.

Chapter Three presents the faunal situation. First an historical reconstruction of what is known about animals in the Selous is developed from both written and oral sources. This is followed by a much more detailed picture of the faunal situation as found during the study period of 1973-1975. It is shown that there is considerable variation in the distribution of wildlife between the wet season and the dry season; furthermore, certain spaces are far more important than others when judged by the density of the wildlife inhabiting them. Those species which show an affinity for the grasslands during the rainy season have very restricted distributions at that time. The woodland creatures are more dispersed.

Chapter Four draws together the physical setting, the human settlement scene, and the wildlife census to illustrate that there seems to be important spatial overlap between human and animal resource preferences. The localities which now contain very high densities of animals coincide with former settlement sites. By way of contrast, the case of active settlement around Horowe Village shows the opposite. There is a clear avoidance of a site until it is abandoned by humans; at the time of abandonment, animals take up occupancy of the area. Several disturbance mechanisms which might operate to exclude animals from settled areas are discussed and discarded as inadequate explanations of the observed phenomenon.

The conclusion is that the work supports the thesis that the presence of humans depressed some large mammal species' populations. It is quite possible that the mere presence of active human settlement was sufficient to accomplish this because it coincided with the presence of critical resources and was associated with disturbance which was avoided by most animals. It is further suggested that there is little reason to assume that certain species were negatively affected by the human presence.

The research as presented focuses quite narrowly on the problem of overlapping space requirements of people and wildlife. Viewed in other ways it has much broader implications and has a practical aspect in the context of Tanzania today. Much of the country is being reorganized into radically new settlement patterns that concentrate human populations into quite small spaces. Until now, attention has centered on the places receiving the influx of reorganized peoples.

This investigation looks at an area which was abandoned in a manner not unlike many areas are being abandoned today. The colonial government incorporated thousands of square miles into the Selous Game Reserve in order to insure that people would not slowly reinhabit the abandoned expanses. In so doing, they successfully prohibited recolonization while at the same time providing a wildlife sanctuary. The result was a game reserve large enough to be ecologically complete, and a human population which was a bit more accessible to modernizing forces in the country. Expansion of certain reserves might reinforce this process today.

This study also provides an inventory of the wildlife resource in one location, a description of its distribution, and therefore the basis on which to build a wildlife development plan. Such a plan would be complementary to the development plans which already exist for the newly settled areas.

Chapter I

THE SELOUS GAME RESERVE IN ITS GEOGRAPHICAL
AND HISTORICAL CONTEXT

The Location of the Selous

Tanzania is one of the poorest countries in the world. Nevertheless, it has valued its wildlife heritage enough to spend considerable amounts of energy and money to preserve it. An estimated 25% of the country is protected as game estate where the killing of animals is either forbidden (National Parks) or allowed under limited permit systems which are controlled by the Game Division (Game Reserves and Controlled Areas). Except for controlled areas, settlement is generally forbidden in these expansive pieces of territory.

The Selous Game Reserve is the largest of these game areas and occupies a substantial portion of southeastern Tanzania. It is situated in an area of only moderate rainfall with the rain gauge at the Miombo Research Centre[1] recording an average of 30 inches (800 millimetres) over a six year period. The extreme variability and seasonality of the rains is illustrated by Figure 2. The temperature extremes recorded thus far range from a high of 106 degrees Fahrenheit (41° C.) in December to a low of 56 degrees (13° C.) in June.

The vegetation forms which have evolved under these regimes of temperature and rainfall range from dense thickets to open wooded grasslands. In localized areas treeless grasslands exist, but are usually the result of edaphic wetness. Rodgers and Ludanga (1973) have given a detailed description including species lists for a part of the Eastern Selous which they mapped using 16 categories of vegetation types. The more casual observer would see two major divisions in vegetation as he traverses the reserve. The eastern one-sixth is a wooded grassland characterized by picturesque flat topped trees (Terminalia spinosa).

---

[1] For most place names in the Selous see Figure 1.

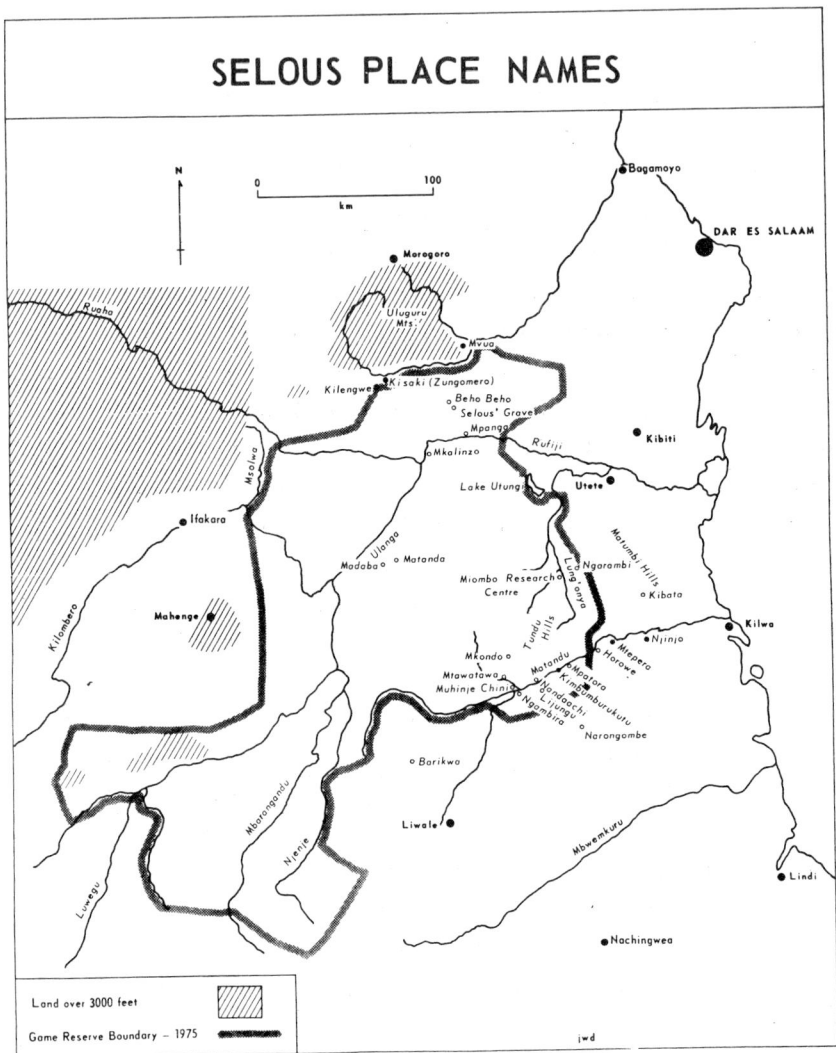

FIGURE 1

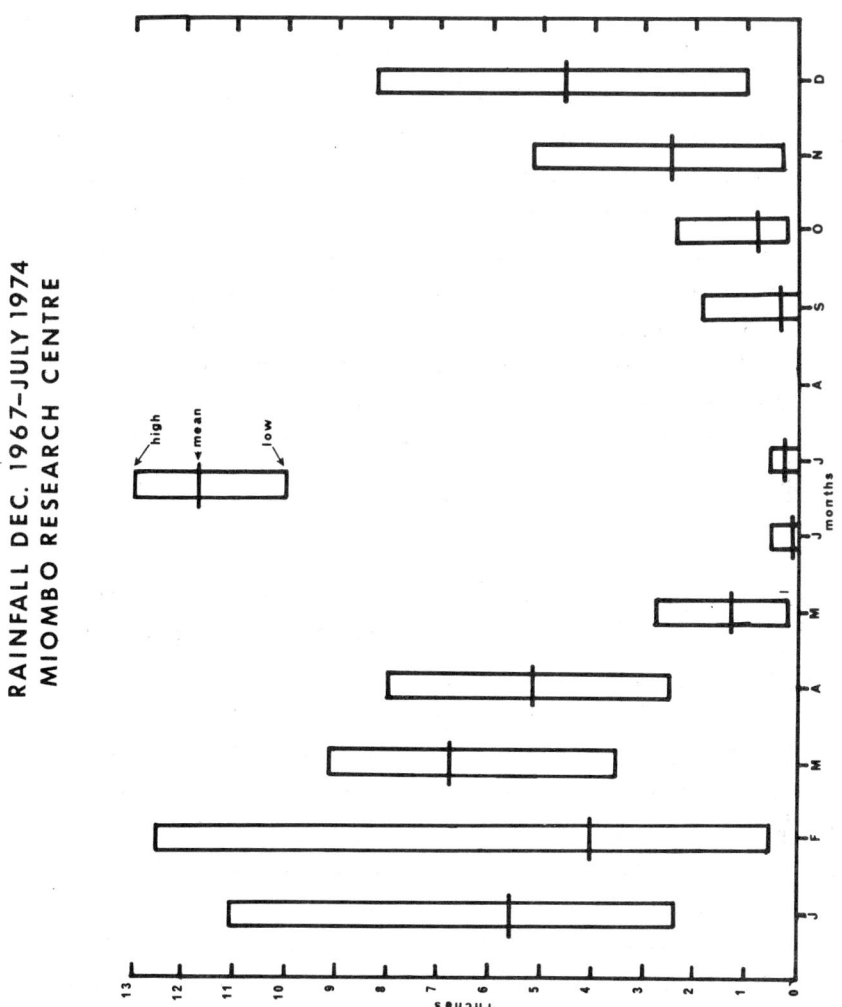

FIGURE 2. THE RAINFALL REGIME AT THE MIOMBO RESEARCH CENTRE.

Within this area, which is considerably more open than the rest of the Selous, there exist the only cheetah and giraffe to be found in the reserve. As elsewhere in African grassland locations, large numbers of plains game are often concentrated. To the west, the deciduous miombo (Brachystegia) woodland predominates.[1] Here plains game are scattered about in small clusters usually corresponding to open stretches along drainage lines.[2] To the extreme south and west of the reserve wildebeest and impala all but disappear. The miombo is particularly favorable habitat for elephant, Lichtenstein's harteheest and sable antelope.

The entire Selous is tsetse infested and three different species of this fly have been recorded (Glossina morisitans, G. pallipides, G. brevipalpis), (Atlas, 1967). The presence of the fly has protected the reserve from encroachment by the cattle-keeping people who range over much of the game estate in the northern parts of the country. Likewise, the sleeping sickness transmitted by tsetse played an important role in prompting the removal of all humans from the reserve.

The lands within the reserve never supported high densities of human population, and just prior to the human exodus the density figure probably did not exceed 2-1/2 people per square mile (.8 p. km^2). (Matzke, 1971a). A recently uncovered 1931 estimate for the Liwale area which included much of the reserve put the figure at about 2 people p.s.m. (.8 p.km^2) (File 22/3). Even today most territory bordering the game reserve is devoid of people. The closest population concentrations of note are along the mountains to the north and west as well as in the Rufiji Valley to the east (Fig. 3).

---

[1] Miombo comes from the Kinyamwezi name "muyombo" which refers to the tree Brachystegia boehmii. Brachystegia is one of the commonest genera in this kind of woodland (Lind and Morrison, 1974).

[2] These drainage lines are often referred to as "dambos" in literature on Brachystegia woodlands. The term is not used by the people in the Selous vicinity.

The general lack of resident people near the reserve has kept it free from the extremely heavy pressures of illegal hunting that threaten many East African wildlife sanctuaries. Until the construction of the Great Uhuru Railway (connecting the Zambian copper belt with Dar es Salaam port) through the Selous (Matzke, 1971b), no all weather transport route even reached its boundaries. Because the terrain is such that movement without prepared routes is difficult, poaching has generally been confined to the borders within a few days walk of the three closest population concentrations mentioned above.

It is a reflection on the paucity of known resources within the reserve to say that to date no substantial part of the entire 21,000 square miles (55,000 km^2) has been seriously sought for alternative uses by development planners. (see Fig. 4) A few thousand acres along the Msolwa River have been taken over for cultivation near the Kilombero Sugar Company and it is possible that further losses will occur there in the future. It is the only irrigable land within the reserve mentioned by an F.A.O. study of the Rufiji Basin (Anderson, 1960). Spence (1957) suggested that this section along with another bordering the Mgeta River were the only places that showed agricultural possibilities. Subsequent development plans for the Mgeta site included only areas outside the reserve (Spooner and Jenkins, 1966).

Part of the Selous has been gazetted as forest reserve (Fig. 4), but no exploitation has taken place to date. It seems unlikely to gain much interest since the value of its produce is not high. Miombo has a low proportion of valuable trees in what is normally a light forest cover (F.A.O., 1961a).

Hopes for mineral production were raised around the turn of the century when thin seams of coal were discovered on the Mshindazi River near its confluence with the Rufiji and also near Mvua just north of the reserve. Later investigation showed the inch thick seams to be worthless. Other geological investigations as recently as 1974 have uncovered no valuable mineral deposits in the Selous.

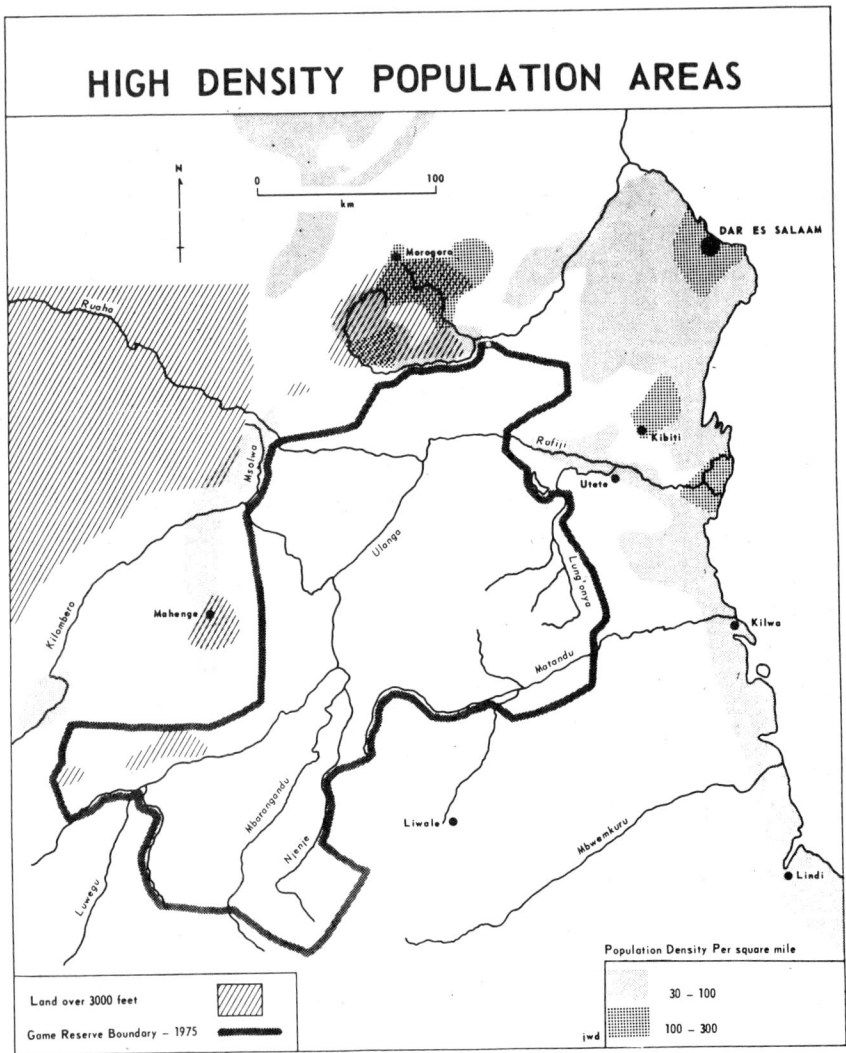

FIGURE 3

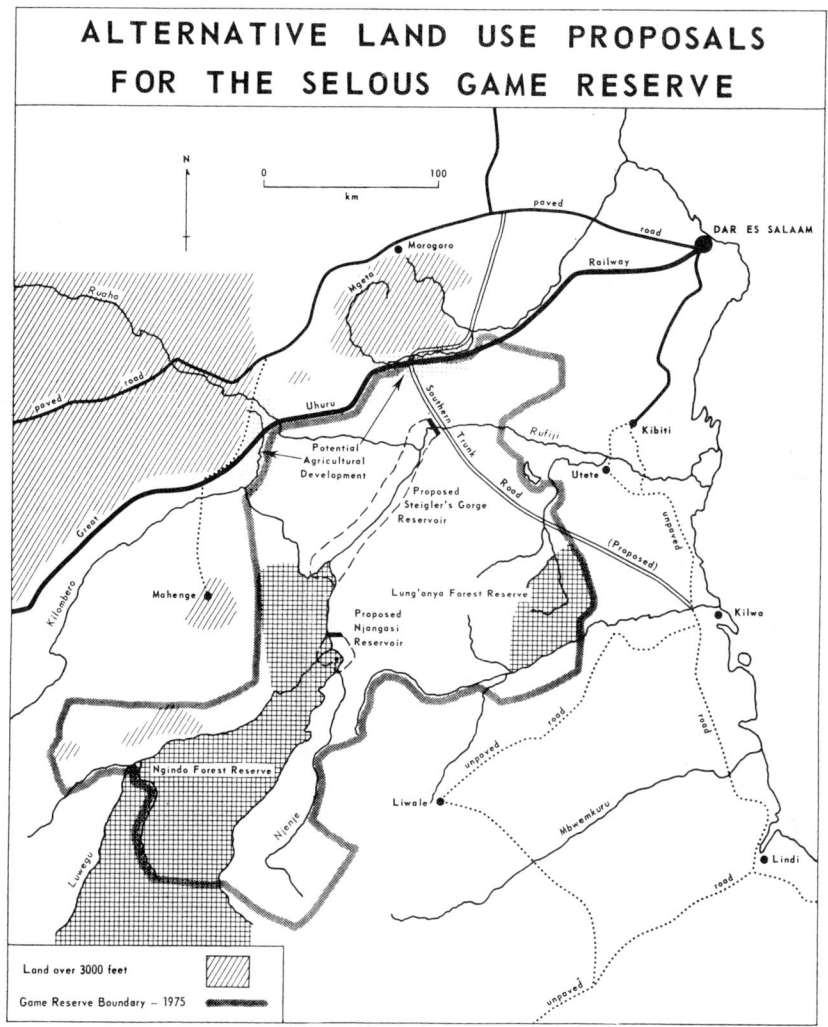

FIGURE 4

There is one proposed development plan whose implementation will change the character of the existing Selous. This aims at harnessing the flood waters of the Rufiji River. An F.A.O. study selected two sites which together with their reservoirs would be entirely within the reserve (Otnes, 1961). These sites located at Stiegler's Gorge and Njangasi would require all weather access routes as well as a resident work force for maintenance and power generation. A survey has been completed for a road to cross atop the proposed dam at Stiegler's Gorge and thereby provide an all weather link to the southern parts of Tanzania (Fig. 4). Such a link would open up the Selous to easy tourist access. The Rufiji floods of 1974 prompted the Tanzanian Government to announce that construction on the dam project would begin by 1980. In the absence of specific financial arrangements, this remains far from a certainty.

Except for its wildlife, the Selous is resource poor. The dams proposed for the Rufiji River system will control waters which arise mainly outside of the Selous for the benefit of people residing some distance away. The electricity will be exported to Dar es Salaam and the agricultural people of the lower Rufiji will be protected from floods. It is the lack of resources and the hostility of its environment which has allowed such a huge expanse of territory to grow into a large game sanctuary without excessive competition from human interests.

With the general location and resource base of the Selous area understood, it is useful to develop a history of the human happenings in the vicinity over the last few centuries. After tracing this history, the emergent settlement pattern can be more clearly brought into focus.

History in the Selous

> This is the "dry forest" of the savannah, usually called <u>miombo</u> in Tanganyika Territory where it covers three-fifths of the land.... During the wet season it is a symphony of green foliage and blue

sky, in spring an orgy of colour from the brightest
gold through orange and red to brown, spread like
a precious eastern carpet over the gentle ridges of
the peneplain, in the drought, after the fires have
swept over the land, that awful and yet beautiful
blending of the blackish grey ashes and grey leaf-
less stems which one can best describe as "the silver
death of the miombo." One must have marched through
its uninhabited and mostly uninhabitable, because
waterless, monotony for weeks, one must have gazed
over tens of thousands of square miles of this forest
from high up in the air, in order to grasp its utter
hopelessness from the point of view of human enter-
prise (Gillman, 1936).

Hopeless is the word most often used to describe the miombo woodland and its development potential. A U.N. study mentioned honey and beeswax production as the primary industry of these woodlands in Tanzania (F.A.O., 1961a). Such products are hardly the stuff that would give optimism to development minded men viewing the vastness of these bushlands. Yet, for centuries scattered groups of people have managed to live throughout the three million square miles of miombo in south central Africa.[1] While these lands never gave birth to any of the great African civilizations, they did provide a stage for several important events in recent African history. They pro- duced some of the slaves and much of the ivory that stimulated early trade to the interior. Their tsetse killed off all pack animals and thereby reduced man to the beast of burden for early European explorers. Finally, this was the stage where many of the dramas of the Maji-Maji and World War I were acted out.

The dispersed residents of the miombo in what is now southeastern Tanzania survived the vicissitudes of history and clung to their bush lands until the twentieth century. Bit by

---

[1]The area undoubtedly has a very long history of human occupance, although most of its history has gone unrecorded. Spence (1957) reported finding stone implements of an early unknown people on the Rufiji River above Mkalinzo. On a beach near Kimbumburukutu pool along the Matandu River I found quartz pieces which appeared to be human artifacts. Hibben (1967) investigated one sight at Lukuliro and found numerous implements which he thought to be similar to that of Olduvai (i.e. at least one million years old).

bit, as this century proceeded, three different governments gradually have added to the amount of land forbidden to the aboriginal inhabitants. As a result, today the 21,000 square mile Selous Game Reserve stands as an unpeopled island in a sea of otherwise lightly settled miombo.

Prior to the action by the various governments, however, many forces effectively limited human populations in the Selous area. This sparse settlement pattern was observed in 1616 by a Portuguese explorer who made a journey from Tete to Kilwa and referred to the lands he crossed in southeastern Tanzania as "terra deserta." He made one march of seven days and another of four days without seeing any habitation. He suggested that soil and water conditions were the reason for the dispersed settlement he found (Grey, 1948).

The subsequent accounts of European explorers give clues to both the natural and human scourges that were characteristic of the region. Although quite limited in the amount of the territory they actually traversed, their accounts provide some indications as to the type of human settlement found during the last century. The routes of the nineteenth and early twentieth century explorers through the Selous are shown in Figure 5. Their published observations of these journeys provide most of the written evidence available for understanding the recent past of the people living in the Selous area. The following discussion of this history necessarily relies heavily on these accounts.

Observers from the mid-nineteenth century until the present agree on one thing: the inhabitants of the Selous and its environs always lived in small settlements separated by considerable expanses of uninhabited bush. This is particularly interesting since there were a number of different peoples represented in the area (Fig. 6) and in a number of locations the resource base could have sustained larger numbers of agricultural people. In 1878, Joseph Thomson observed this and commented with reference to the Kutu in the northern Selous:

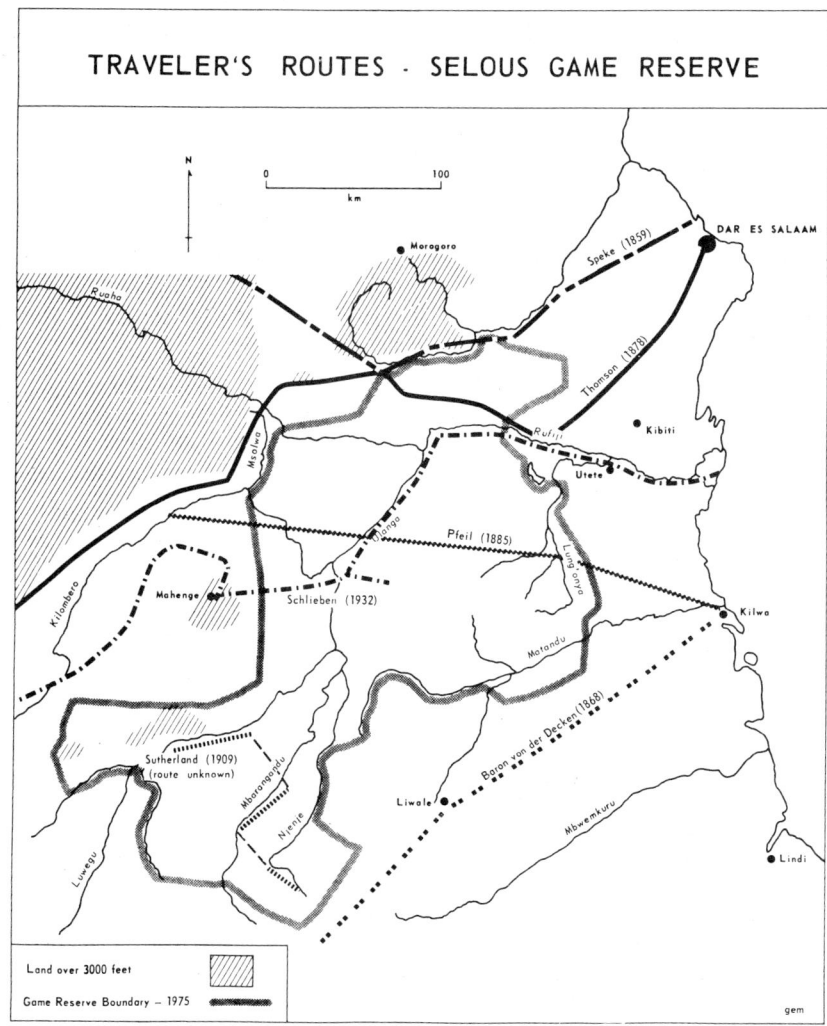

FIGURE 5

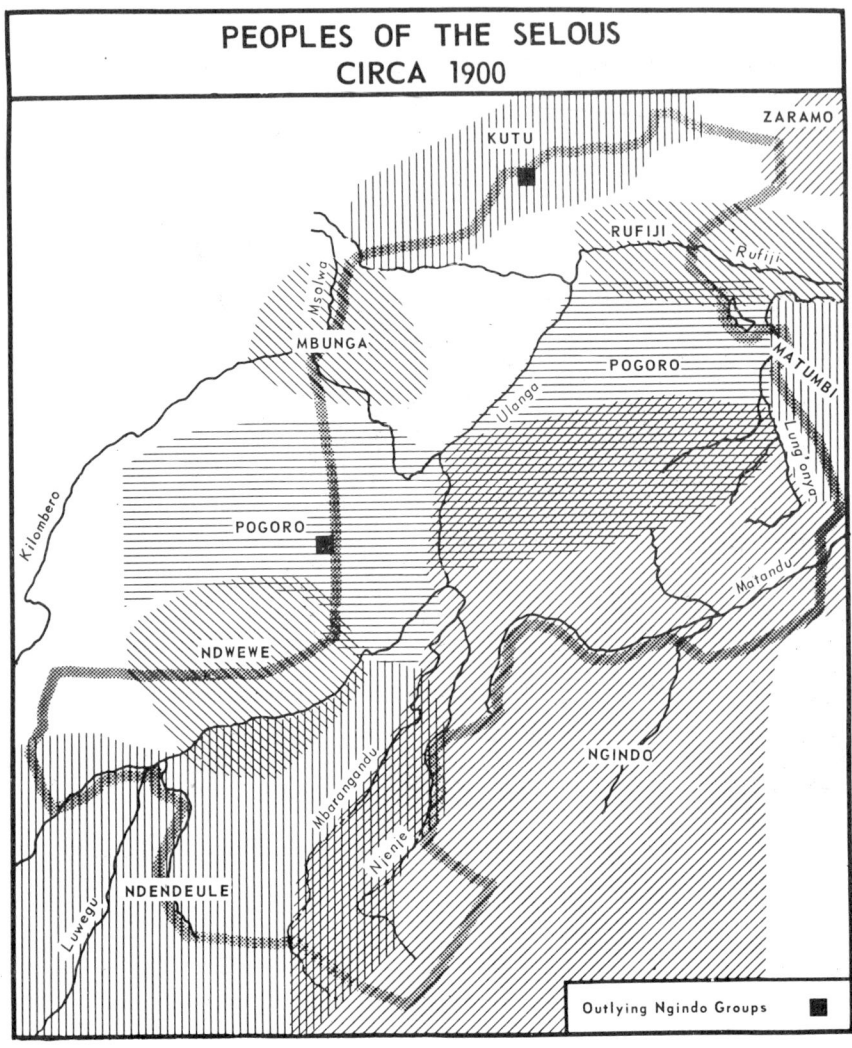

FIGURE 6

> Now among the Wakhutu (sic) there is no common
> union for protection. A few families perhaps
> collect together and settle down in a village
> and nominally recognize a headman among them;
> but with individuals of other villages they have
> no common action or mutual dependence. Hence,
> when an enemy appears requiring the whole strength
> of the tribe to cope with him, there are no means
> of securing unity or common action. Each village
> has to depend on itself, and there is nothing for
> it but to flee for their lives into the jungles
> and forest (Thomson, 1968, p. 161).

A later observer has generalized about the small group societies of southern Tanzania. He said that "Political organizations based on lineage and clan were widely scattered all over the country although they were largely concentrated in southern Tanzania. In these societies there were no large political units since inter-clan loyalty did not usually transcend clan allegiance (Kimambo and Temu, 1969, p. 89)."

The result of this lack of an effective tribal superstructure was predictable. The small bush villages were favorite targets for the more powerful forces that were continually sweeping through the region.

Perhaps the most powerful and long lasting force creating chaos was the slave trade. Since the middle ages numerous reports exist showing Kilwa to be a major exporter of both slaves and ivory.[1] Major caravan routes to the interior branched out from Kilwa to Kisaki, Ifakara and Liwale on their way to the interior of Africa.

Baron von der Decken (1871) traveled the southern most of these routes inland from Kilwa for about two hundred miles (320 kilometres) in 1860. He noted that the country he passed through was thickly populated in spots and generally peaceful.

---

[1] For extensive review of these the reader is referred to Crosse-Upcott, 1956, p. 389 and following.

According to his observations, the slaves passing along this route came from much farther up-country. Although this was generally the case, the concentration of slave routes in southeastern Tanzania facilitated the periodic uptake of slaves from there as well.

The slave trade was intensified after the transfer of the Omani Arab realm's center to Zanzibar in 1840. This turned Kilwa into the largest slave emporium on the whole coast. By the mid-1800s, possibly 10,000 slaves a year were exported from Kilwa (Crosse-Upcott, 1956).

The record leaves little doubt that slavery was a way of life when the first Europeans visited Zungomero (now Kisaki) just north of the present day Selous boundary in 1857. This was the junction between two major slave and ivory trade routes and during the travelling season large caravans of some thousand men passed through it every week (Richards, 1960).

The spin off of these slave routes reached into the villages of Ukutu. Burton observed:

> The same attractions which draw caravans to Zungomero render it the great rendevous of an army of touters, who, whilst watching for the arrival of the ivory traders, amuse themselves with plundering the country. The plague has now spread like a flight of locusts over the land. The Wa'khutu (sic), a timid race, who unlike the Wazaramo, have no sultan to gather round, are being gradually ousted from their ancient seats. In a large village there will seldom be more than three or four families, who occupy the most miserable hovels, all the best having been seized by the touters or pulled down for firewood. These men--slaves, escaped criminals, and freemen of broken fortunes, flying from misery, punishment, or death on the coast are armed with muskets and sabres, bows and spears, daggers and knobsticks.... If money runs short, a village is fired by night, and the people are sold off to the first caravan (Burton, 1860, pp. 97-8).

One village, Kilengwe, then in Kutuland and now in the game reserve, was visited at least three times over a twenty year period by Europeans. Burton had camped there with Speke on their return journey from central Africa. On his next journey only a short time later, Speke scheduled a stop for resupply at this same village. He was, however, disappointed since the place was deserted. "The slave hunters had driven every vestige of humanity away (Speke, 1864, p. 64)." It was at this spot eighteen years later that Joseph Thomson rested for three days and recorded that since Burton had first passed through Kutuland "their (Kutu) material condition had certainly improved." He said that since slavery had become a way of life[1] the people had "emerged from their hiding places amongst marshes and jungles" and now lived in villages of two or three hundred houses situated in impregnable tracts of forest (Thomson, 1968, p. 159).

Not all was restored in Ukutu. Several days later on the Msendasi in the northwestern Selous area Thomson saw evidence of past cultivation that had not yet regained its past splendor. At that time he wrote:

> The valley is about thirty miles long by six to eight miles broad. It is extremely fertile, and watered by numerous streams. The only part now cultivated or inhabited is the extreme northern end, the rest having been laid waste by the Mahenge (Mbunga) who have thus transformed a perfect garden into a desert. So completely have these savages done their work, that, where once were thriving villages, not even a pathway exists through the jungle grass (Thomson, 1968, pp. 168-9).

Thus Thomson introduces the second important element involved in the decimation of the dispersed villages in the Selous country. Intertribal warfare continually created trouble for the clan-centered societies of southern Tanzania in the latter

---

[1] Although commercial slavery was discontinued during the last century, the intertribal and interclan kidnapping of people continued until much later. Many informants alive today report that it was well into English rule before one would dare venture alone away from his village for fear of being captured. The chiefs appointed by the English often took it upon themselves to send men into other chiefdoms to capture and bring back people they felt should be under their jurisdiction. The Ngindo of Liwale and Ulanga districts continually crossed the district borders for this purpose until the 1940s. The files of the colonial government are filled with correspondence on such matters.

half of the nineteenth century. "This turbulent era... brought sudden death, famine, or enslavement to so many.... (Hallett, 1970, p. 406)."

Thomson's safari ran into a war party of Mahenge (Mbunga) that had passed north of the Rufiji on their way to raid the Waluguru to the north. It is not certain why people from a fertile homeland should have found it necessary to continually sweep out and raid the Kutu and the Luguru, but traditional accounts emphasize that they came because of famine (Brain, 1968). The Mahenge were the northern most offshoot of a much larger movement of Ngoni people. As the forward elements of the Ngoni armies migrated from the south through the Ubena Valley, they robbed and pillaged as they swept through the bottomlands. As was common elsewhere in southern Tanzania, there was little effective resistance. These lowlands had been a refuge for

> fugitives from the higher country all around who had sought the inaccessible swamps as a hiding place from the warrior tribes by whom they were surrounded. Each community was a law unto itself, living in watery isolation and taking to the densest parts of the swamps when danger threatened (Culwick and Culwick, 1935, p. 22)."

As the Ngoni spearhead moved north, a chief from Ubena of the hills, Mtengera, sent help to harrassed valley people. He thus drove a wedge between the main Ngoni tribe and the splinter group which had moved to the north. This cut off retreat and reinforcement. As a result, these people settled down in the lower part of the Kilombero valley, but before stopping they fought all over the Morogoro Region and reached as far as Bagamoyo. Since they had come from near a hill called Mbunga in Ngoniland, they adopted that as their tribal name.[1]

Although the Mahenge raids were an important factor in disrupting life in the northern section, their powerful Ngoni

---

[1] They are often called Mafiti or Mahenge in early records.

relatives proved to be a more widespread affliction for the people of southern Tanzania in the last half of the nineteenth century (Hallet, 1970). After their leader died in Ufipa in 1845, they split into two groups. The southern group swept through the Songea region and beyond. Here was a place devoid of strong political organizations that might have halted their advance. Rather, the clan allegiance system of the scattered peoples in the south provided a vacuum through which the Ngoni moved at will. For these people the Ngoni raids brought utter destruction.

The Ngoni raids were widespread. Figure 7 is an attempt to illustrate the general picture as well as some of the specific locations of conflicts gleaned from numerous published and oral accounts.

Of the Selous inhabitants, the Ngindo probably suffered the most of any people since they were in the mainstream of the Ngoni thrusts toward Kilwa. Indeed, "The Ngindo to this day speak with bitter memory of the havoc and terror wrought by Ngoni ravages (Kimambo and Temu quoting Gwassa 1969, p. 88)."

Many Ngindo were captured by the Ngoni and amalgamated into their tribe. Two major groups claiming to be Ngoni (Ndendeule and Mbunga) actually speak a dialect of the Ngindo language. It seems certain that as many groups before them, they adopted some of the ways of their conquerors and changed their ethnic identification in the process (Crosse-Upcott, 1956).

The Ngindo living in the open valleys, in villages, or along regularly traveled routes were especially vulnerable to the periodic sweeps of Ngoni raiders. Many found their best defense was to flee. Some fled considerable distances and pockets of them are still found anywhere from Lake Nyasa to the coast between the Uluguru Mountains and the Ruvuma River. The mass of their population shifted north and east from their starting point in Ndendeule country northeast of Songea (Crosse-Upcott, 1956). Within this area, centered on Liwale but extending throughout much of the southern Selous, they dispersed into the plateau thickets. Here they were afforded a measure of

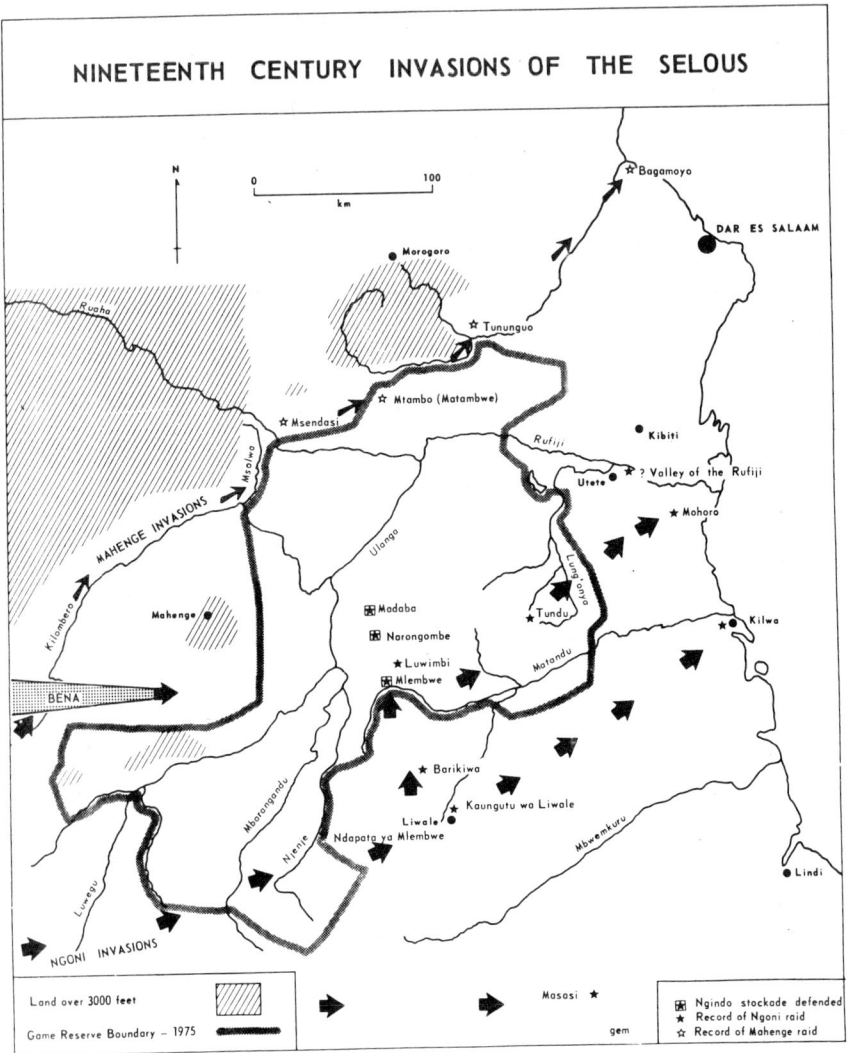

FIGURE 7

protection by their isolation. No villages worthy of the name could be found in Ngindoland. Rather, the inhabitants maximized distance between themselves and their neighbors. As Crosse-Upcott (1956, p. 423) put it "If the slave trade was the instigator of Ngindo pulverizations, the Ngoni were its executioners."

Some measure of the anguish caused by the Ngoni can be seen by the fact that the Ngindo of Liwale sent mwenye[1] Mpinga to Kilwa to ask the Germans for aid in repulsing Ngoni attacks. The Germans responded by building a fort at Barikwa and chastening the Ngoni (Bell, 1950).

The invitation to the Germans seemed a way out of the turmoil caused by outsiders. Such was not the case. In a short time the Ngoni terror was replaced by the tyranny of the Germans. Today the Ngindo describe the switch from Ngoni to German oppression as "Wanatoka wafako, wanakwenda wazikwako" (They go from where there is death to where there is burial) (Bell, 1950, p. 55).

The German government implemented policies aimed at the production of cash crops in southern Tanzania. In particular, cotton was introduced by means of both government and private plantations. In both cases, labor was conscripted to work on plantations with a decrease in time available for private cultivation. The punishment for failure to willingly come forward for work was a severe lashing at the hands of the overseers. The cotton system was, in terms of labor and physical suffering, imposing impossible demands on many Africans.

The agents of this oppression during German times usually were the German askaris[2] who enjoyed and abused their unbridled

---

[1] Mwenye is a Swahili title used for a period of time in the early colonial rule. It might read as designated official, i.e. headman.

[2] This is a term which is used to refer to anyone performing a military, police, or guard duty. In this case, it refers to African soldiers and police attached to the various colonial administrative headquarters and used to enforce government policy directives.

power, "The set policy of the government was to introduce as many foreign elements as possible among their native troops and the terror which these men inspired was hideous (Bell, 1950, p. 55)."

The headmen (jumbes) of the scattered villages were the least immune to terror. When an agent of the government came to his village he was to bear the burden of all forthcoming requests. One author recounts:

> An askari did not make a request for so many fowls, men for labour, or whatever else he required; he took these things and a good many more by force. Arriving at a village close to that of the jumbe to whom he had been sent he would call the nearest native and issue instructions. Producing a cartridge from his pouch he would tell the native to take it to the jumbe who must be ordered to prepare four beds, one for the askari, one for his rifle, one for his ammunition pouch and one for his clothes. The final order was always the same - a blanket with which to cover the askari. By this was meant, and was always understood to be, a woman to the askari's liking and it went ill with any jumbe who failed to provide all these requirements (Bell, 1950, p. 55).

As more and more were awarded doses of "hamsa ishirini" (twenty lashes) for real and imagined offenses against the German government and its representatives, resentment grew in the southern part of the new German colony.

In July of 1905, the first signs of rebellion appeared among the Matumbi. The seminal incident was reaction to an order for the local people to start picking cotton at Kibata. Upon the advice of a powerful medicine man, Bokero, from Ngarambi, the people resisted. Within two months, the people in a hundred thousand square miles of Africa were in revolt (Bell, 1950).

The revolt moved immediately into the area of the Selous. Bokero's powerful medicine water was dispensed from his village on the Lungonya River (now the eastern boundary of the Selous) and its strength gave courage to the discontented living elsewhere. Another "doctor" distributed water with a similar magic power from Mpanga on the Rufiji River (Bell, 1950). Soon foreign elements were attacked and killed by the Pogoro at Madaba and the Ngindo at Liwale (Fig. 8).

Amazingly, the war spread through an area of vast extent that had previously known no political unity. Interclan loyalty usually did not transcend clan allegiance, but as the Hongo (medicine man couriers) from one village brought news and magic water to the next, the clan political units of the south gave the Germans nightmares. The Maji-Maji rebellion soon became the most widespread threat to German rule in East Africa (Kimambo and Temu, 1969).

The German government began a systematic suppression of the movement by November of 1905 and martial law was lifted in August of 1907. Most of the fighting took place in the very beginning as the insurgents soon tasted the machine gun fire of a strong force that spent three weeks near Madaba during the end of 1905. With over 900 men in one force, the demands for food were considerable. The lightly settled woodlands were scoured and the Maji-Maji food stores suffered accordingly (Bell, 1950).

One interviewee recalled: "the famine of the Maji-Maji was worse than all others. We were in hiding from the soldiers and didn't have time to cultivate for three years." (Pamunda Interview, 1974).

Aside from the food taken to supply the armies, much more was lost to the torch. The Germans succeeded in quelling the rebellion after the implementation of a scorched-earth policy. The resulting famine killed hundreds of thousands in southern German East Africa (Clyde, 1962).

The Germans employed their scorched-earth policy with such thoroughness that there were no seeds left for planting new crops after the war. One man described the situation thusly:

> There came three years' famine. Those who survived did so by Providence. It was extremely fierce famine and people denied their children and wives.... There has never been the like either before or after Maji-Maji. People died in multitudes... and lions (wild

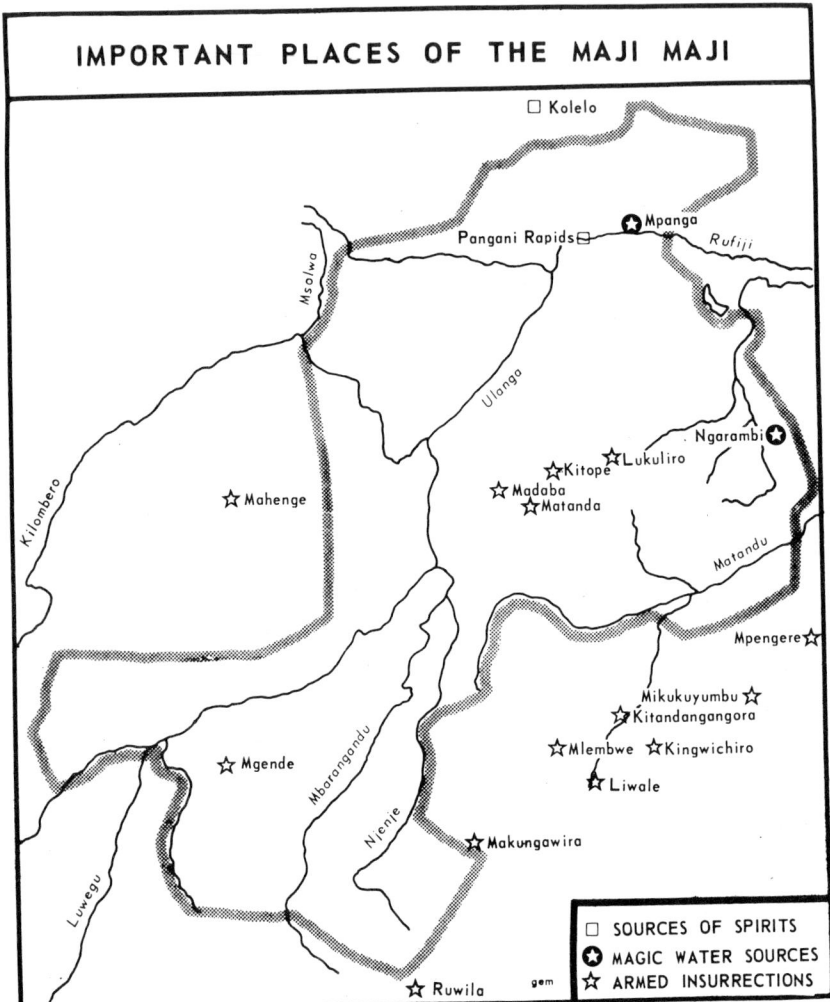

FIGURE 8

animals) ate one after the other (Gwassa and Iliffe quoting Kiango, 1967, pp. 27-8).

The populace suffered such a blow from the Maji-Maji that they never again were able to regain their former numbers, sparse as they were originally. In the Matumbi Hills, a well watered location just east of the Selous Reserve:

> Before the war the population was very dense and it was difficult to find a piece of land on which to grow food. If you got a small piece of land you thanked God--there were too many people. Now, alas, you see much bush everywhere (Gwassa and Iliffe quoting Kiango, 1967, p. 28).

The scars of the Maji-Maji had but seven years to heal before war once again came to German East Africa. The war was slow in reaching the southeastern part as the initial fighting was centered near the northern borders with British controlled territory. Residents report that their first involvement came when each sub-chief (jumbe mdogo) was requested to supply ten young men to "go to war." A hundred soldiers were thus recruited from the Madaba vicinity. As the war progressed this procedure was repeated three times (Kujogopa interview, 1974).

In September of 1916, the German army main force retreated south of the central railway line at Morogoro. They established defensive positions along the Mgeta River which now forms the northern Selous boundary. The clashes in that area were indecisive and the vastly outnumbered German forces were able to keep the allied forces from advancing on that front for three months.

The position of the opposing armies in September 1916 is shown in Figure 9. The German lines were in a horseshoe shape with the Selous in the center. Since all access to the sea was cut off, the burden for their support fell on the meager resources of the local inhabitants. In the German rear, the peasant grain stores were gathered into magazines which could supply troops as they retreated. Two major magazines were set up at Madaba and Liwale with minor stores elsewhere.[1]

Levies were apportioned to headmen and sub-headmen in turn organized the collection of food from the people in their respective areas. The women were pressed into service to prepare flour from the collected grain. Stories still abound to the hardships this imposed as they worked until their hands were raw and bleeding. To facilitate the preparation of flour, hundreds of men were conscripted to drag a steam operated milling machine from Kilwa to Madaba. Upon arrival the women were released from their task of pounding grain.[2] In other places the populace worked continually until the retreat of the Germans. In order to avoid this hardship, many people simply abandoned their homesteads and fled into the bush and thereby continued the traditional defensive posture established by their forefathers.

The German strategy was aimed at keeping large numbers of the enemy occupied without ever really engaging in decisive combat. Thus they held the Mgeta front long enough to use up all their supplies while the allies struggled to build up their stocks by laboriously hauling supplies through the Uluguru Mountains. When they were ready for the attack, they found only rearguard German units. The German main force had crossed the Rufiji and cleaned out all the foodstocks of that fertile valley, and the flooded river was between themselves and the enemy. The allied forces once again had to be resupplied from the rear while the German forces planted hundreds of acres of crops around Lake Utungi and waited in the rain for the harvest. This was done because there were so few people in the area to

---

[1] Old residents who witnessed the events report a small store at Matanda and a somewhat larger one at Mpatora (Jiwe la Obasi). (Interviews with Kujogopa and Keusi).

[2] This machine can still be seen near Nambarapi south of Madaba where it was reportedly abandoned during an air attack on the retreating Germans. In any case, its slow progress could not keep pace with the retreating German forces.

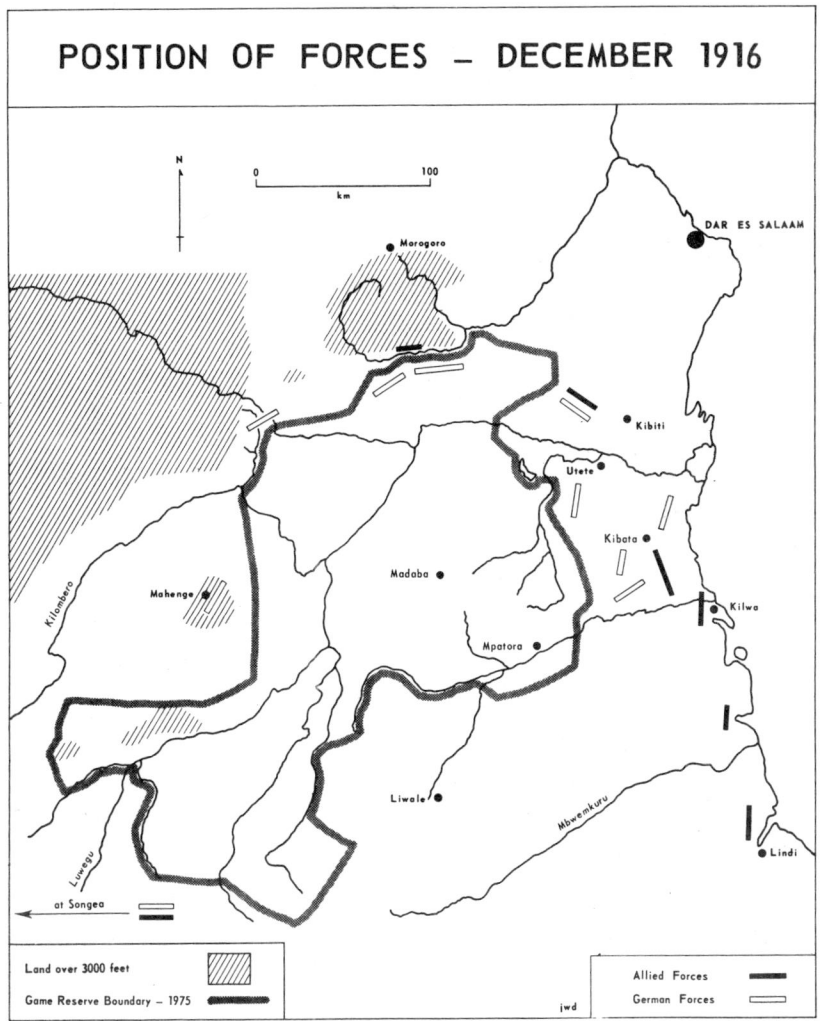

FIGURE 9

supply them. When an allied force threatened the German rear from Kilwa, it was diverted into action in the Matumbi Hills near Kibata where the terrain and supply difficulties bogged it down. Just before the German crops were ready, some 5000 porters were sent over to the allied forces to conserve on food supplies (Lettow-Vorbeck, 1918).

The ripening of the crops coincided with the end of the rains so the German forces collected their food and beat a hasty retreat from Lake Utungi to Mpatora and then out of the Selous (Fig. 10). Their position was advantageous, being near the drier headwaters of the rivers. The allied forces, in contrast, were downstream on the coast and along the Rufiji River, still mired in the mud and in constant need of resupply from the rear.

The arrival of the allied forces was welcomed by the people who had suffered under the German occupation. For the first time in a year they could go to the coast to buy salt and other trade goods (Kujogopa Interview, 1974). The mandatory carrying of 60 kg (132 pounds) war loads had hardly been an easy task for those engaged as porters (Lamden, 1963). The attempts to recruit porters at Kisaki were summarily unsuccessful. "The numerous inhabitants, to whom the war and the many askaris (soldiers) were something quite new, lost their heads and ran into the bush." (Gardner, p. 111).

Although few non-combatants died during World War I, the demands of the German forces once again reinforced the wisdom of those who chose to flee and live an isolated existence in the thickets and elsewhere. Anyone who lived in a more agglomerated settlement was readily available to perform the tasks demanded by any representative of the occupying powers.

The passing of the armies left the populace without food supplies and in a state of famine. However, in sharp contrast to the Maji-Maji upheavals, they were immediately able to return to their agricultural tasks without fear of reprisal. Within one year the famine had ended and reports do not indicate that it caused many deaths.

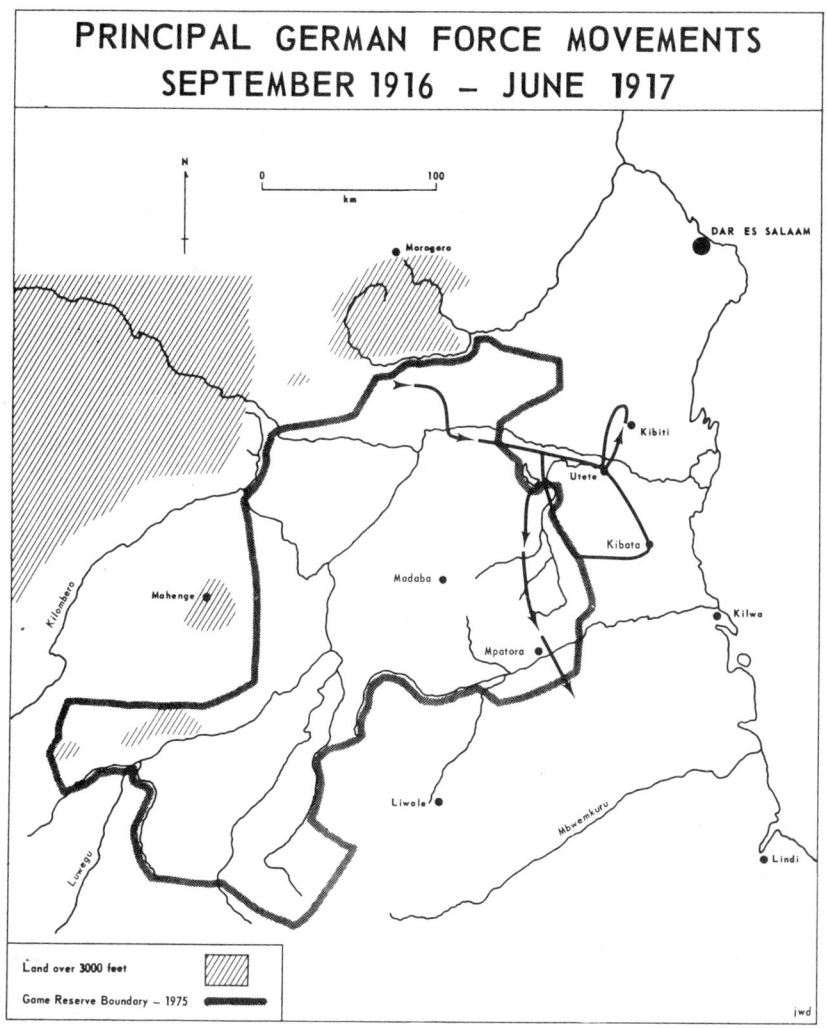

FIGURE 10

The legacies of World War I include a number of sites still bearing the scars of war (see Appendix A in Matzke, 1975 for a complete list) and the name of the game reserve. Captain F. C. Selous, the African naturalist-explorer, died in a skirmish with the German rear guard and his grave can still be seen near Beho Beho in the game reserve which still bears his name.

Prior to World War I, German medical personnel found cases of sleeping sickness near the junction of the Matandu and Liwale Rivers. In 1924, and again in 1936, epidemics occurred in the same area (61/104). A medical officer visiting the scene reported that:

> Inquiry among the more intelligent natives elicited the fact that this type of outbreak has occurred before, not once, but frequently in the past. Their usual remedy being to remove the village, when it started, the disease usually disappeared. The places where it has previously occurred are naturally looked upon with considerable suspicion and left alone, even though water and soil happen to be unusually good. (61/104).

Table 1 supports his contention. Of eleven villages involved in the 1924-1925 sleeping sickness epidemic, six had completely disappeared by 1936. Only two had gained population while three others suffered substantial reductions in size.

The people in this area reacted to natural scourges in the same manner as they did to threats from human quarters. They abandoned their homes and took up a new life elsewhere. However, one could not so easily avoid the events set into motion by the 1936 epidemic. Sleeping sickness really took hold in the Madaba area and in spite of a general quarantine the disease spread until cases were being reported throughout the Southern and Eastern Provinces in the 1940s.

It is useful to examine the reasons for the spread of sleeping sickness after the 1936 epidemic. Previous outbreaks were apparently only local in extent even without the medical attention that was given the 1936 outbreak. Subtle changes in the settlement pattern had emerged since the last war. The

TABLE ONE

POPULATION CHANGES IN VILLAGES REPORTING SLEEPING SICKNESS CASES DURING THE 1924-1925 EPIDEMIC

Village	Sleeping Sickness			Population[1]		
	Deaths	Others	Total	1925	1936	
1. Muhungo	9	8	17	250	120	
2. Kitecho	3	2	16	225	-	
3. Namaganga	6	12	18	174	x	
4. Muhinji Chini	9	6	15	120	159	These two villages are adjoining.
5. Muhinji Chini-Mtawatawa	-	-	-	-	399	
6. Namabao	42	26	68	115	72	
7. Kiringulla	8	1	9	66	36	
8. Ali Kupawiro	1	5	6	60	x	
9. Muhambia	0	1	1	60	x	
10. Nambrikwe	0	1	1	60	x	
11. Nameno	0	1	1	54	x	
12. Mohoro	1	2	3	52	x	
13. Liwale Chini	0	4	4	39	84	

[1]The 1925 figures are estimates of a sleeping sickness officer on the scene. The 1936 figures are the number of taxpayers multiplied by 3 which is a generous conversion based on the author's comparison of the taxpayer data and population size in the provincial records.

xVillage no longer in existence.

⁻No data available.

Revised from: a report by H. Fairbairn, Sleeping Sickness Officer on tour in Liwale District, November 2, 1936. This report is available in the Tanzania National Archives File 61/104.

turmoil of the previous years had subsided and the people started emerging from their hiding places in the thickets and elsewhere. Although still not gathering together in proper villages, considerable numbers of people took up cultivation along the river valleys.

Peace facilitated the shift to the valleys, but traditional accounts give several reasons for it. These include "push" factors which made the thickets and extreme isolation less attractive and "pull" factors which made the valley settlements with their higher densities more attractive.

The thicket locations had provided refuge from enemies, weedless cultivation for a few seasons after clearing, natural rubber trees which provided a source of cash income, a surfeit of famine foods as a cushion against bad years, a light soil which could be tilled with wooden hoes (mijaa),[1] a general lack of animal pests, relative autonomy from the meddling of government and other authorities, a freedom from epidemic diseases more common in places with higher population densities, and less social conflict and the associated witchcraft which inevitably went with it.

The passage of the twentieth century brought numerous changes which lessened the attractiveness of the isolated thicket existence. In the first place, the thickets themselves were decreasing in size because of the clearing by cultivators. This was especially true in locations near permanent water supplies. Five hour round trips to get water were not uncommon.

The price of wild rubber (found only in the thickets) dropped considerably so the people's ability to get a cash income decreased. The invasion of the thickets by elephants fleeing control schemes ended the relatively pest free existence which had earlier been enjoyed. Protection for crops was

---

[1] This traditional tool was similar to the hoe (jembe) now in use, but it used no metal. The digging part was carved from ebony (mpingu, <u>Dalbergia melanoxylon</u>) and fastened to a wooden handle. Informants say it was not sufficiently strong to dig the heavy soils of the valley bottoms.

only available in the locations the government deemed worthwhile enough to station a game scout of the cultivation protection service. Invariably the government favored valley locations where the population was more concentrated, the areas under cultivation more substantial, and the elephants easier to hunt than in the thickets.

The general availability of iron gave cultivators a tool which would enable them to break the heavy soil in the valley bottoms. The crops which could be cultivated there including maize, rice, and sorghum (mtama) were considered to be far more palatable than the cassava and the types of finger millets (uchanji, uchuweli) which were grown in the thickets. The availability of government relief, commercially available food and a freedom to travel to less troubled areas cushioned the shock of crop failure without resorting to the traditional famine foods found in the thickets.[1]

With the passage of time, the fear of government meddling was tempered by the realization that its demands in the form of taxes were compensated for by its service such as medical care, cultivation protection, famine relief, and roads. Along with these things came the rudiments of a commercial economy. The purchase of salt had formerly necessitated a trip of several months to the coast (44/2/37), but traders began establishing themselves at locations along the roads. By 1938, one administrator observed, "The manner in which native settlements are now establishing themselves alongside the roads throughout the province is one of the most remarkable developments of recent years." (Annual Reports, 1938, p. 67).

The above description shows a gradual rationalization of settlement along valley areas in the miombo. This is not to say that real villages emerged, or that the population was truly dense in these areas. As late as 1956, it was observed that

---

[1] For a discussion of the Ngindo famine foods see Crosse-Upcott, 1958.

"Even where the country is solidly Ngindo, the settlements themselves seldom link up. Ten miles is no uncommon interval between them. Excepting under artificial conditions, Ngindo population density does not exceed three persons to the square mile." (Crosse-Upcott, 1956, p. 5).

Another observer described the scene thusly:

> The typical settlement numbers between 5 and 10 miles. A settlement of 10 men will straggle along a river bank or "mbuga" for a distance of over two miles, grouped in 5 and 6 family groups, each group out of sight and hearing of the next. Owing to the small population and large area there is even in the most closely populated parts ... at least 7 or 8 miles between each settlement and in some places ... twenty or more miles. (44/2/37)

Under the conditions described above, sleeping sickness was nearly impossible to control. Previously, the people had maximized their dispersal potential and thereby minimized the possibility of an outbreak of the disease reaching epidemic proportions. Under the new conditions, population densities were just high enough to be favorable for a rapid spread of the disease. Since the ribbon settlement pattern did nothing to destroy the habitat of the tsetse fly, it was always available as the vector for sleeping sickness. After the human population density had increased, there was an improved chance that a fly biting an infected person would find a second person to whom he could transmit the disease.

Initially attempts were made to isolate the outbreak in the vicinity of Madaba. A dispensary with over fifty huts to accommodate families was staffed by personnel trained in the diagnosis and treatment of the disease. Sleeping sickness staff made regular safaris to all of the villages in the area to check and treat new cases. In addition, all travel through the area was banned and an airstrip was constructed in 1937 so that medical and administrative officers could visit the affected area without exposing large numbers of porters to infection. (Annual Reports, 1937) Liaison camps were "established at Muhinje Juu for the importation of salt and cloth and the exportation of native produce." This was done in order to "discourage the people from breaking the quarantine and going to the coast.... in search of these commodities." (61/104) Letters were brought out by the government messenger and posted free of charge. A game scout was assigned to protect the crops and provide free game meat. All people who contracted the disease or whose income or condition of living was negatively affected by the quarantine were excused from paying taxes.

The outbreak of sleeping sickness in the Madaba area persisted. Finally, it was decided to concentrate the populace into a "closer settlement." This was the first attempt at such a concentration in the type of country found in southeastern Tanzania, although it had been tried with considerable success elsewhere (1/102).

The theory behind the concentration of people into compact areas is simple. Generally speaking, the more open the country, the less suitable it is as a breeding habitat for tsetse flies which require shade (Langlands, 1967). Tsetse usually will not cross cleared barriers of a mile or two in width. Since it would be impractical to maintain a cleared strip of this width around isolated hamlets, the hamlets are consolidated into one location. In this location, the juxtapositioning of fields keeps some areas fly free and a cooperative effort of bush clearing can completely free the remainder of tsetse infestation. With no vectors available to transmit the disease, the continuation of the sleeping sickness cycle is impossible and the disease disappears.

The sleeping sickness authorities recommended that initial densities of 80-100 families per square mile (31-39 p. km^2) were advisable in the concentration areas. This could gradually be reduced to 40 families per square mile (15 p. km^2) as reclamation progressed (1/102). New concentrations of less than 1,000 families were considered unsatisfactory since it was unlikely that more than 25 acres (10 hectares) per family could be maintained bush free in miombo country (22/5). Settlements which were of the "ribbon type" were to be avoided in favor of those growing equally in all directions from a center point.

The adjustments necessary to fulfill the requirements of a successful "closer settlement" would have required a virtual revolution in the lives of the people. To cooperate would have meant:

1. abandoning homesteads with all the accoutrements of houses, fields, and ancestral burying grounds.

2. living in close proximity with people who had another language and culture. The densities would be up to one hundred times that of the traditional situation.

3. giving up their "nomadic cultivation" practices whereby they moved to completely new locations whenever the clan head thought it desirable to do so.

4. submitting to the authority of someone outside the family and cooperating with others in nontraditional activities such as clearing tsetse barriers on a regular and sustained basis.

5. opening up their lives to close scrutiny by the government and thereby being available and subject to the consequences of every administrator's whim and rule.

By 1943, only three years after its establishment, the local District Commissioner wrote:

> The whole working of this concentration is thoroughly unsatisfactory, orders are seldom carried out, and the food position is bad, no clearing is done except under extreme pressure (22/3).

The "closer settlement" at Madaba was a failure and it proved impossible to police the movements of people. Sleeping sickness had spread far from Madaba by 1944. In response to the grave threat to public health caused by the continuing spread of this disease, it was decided that thousands of square miles of miombo country had to be abandoned and all of the people moved into closer settlements of sufficient size to be effective. The general picture of the evacuations from the Selous is shown on Figure 11.

In the original plan, most of southeastern Tanzania was to be emptied of people. Because of a war-caused shortage of transport, delays were inevitable and the actual implementation dragged on for over a decade. With virtual control of sleeping sickness in many areas by the end of the decade (61/504/1) and the announcement of the grandiose groundnuts scheme, many areas to the southeast of the Selous never completed the "closer settlement" program.

The history of the people in the area under study was completed with their removal to the closer settlement schemes. A decade later as the disintegration of these schemes progressed, it was impossible for many people to return to their ancestral lands. When they had moved out of these areas, a new authority had moved in. In order to prevent their return to large areas of tsetse bush, these lands had been added to the country's game estate and all settlement was forbidden. The expansion of the Selous Game Reserve had coincided with the depopulation of huge areas of southeastern Tanzania.[1]

The 1977 boundaries of the Selous Game Reserve mask a lot of the dynamics which created them. The foregoing discussion sketched some of the major events that contributed to the complete elimination of human rights of occupance and the creation of a game sanctuary of unprecedented size. The absence of any known valuable agricultural or mineral resources kept this portion of southern Tanzania free from powerful economic interests which might have challenged game reserve expansion. The human population densities were never substantial, and were continually buffeted by calamitous invasions which further decimated their numbers. A serious outbreak of sleeping sickness

---

[1] A detailed history of the evolution of the Selous Game Reserve itself is available in Matzke, 1975 and Matzke, 1976b.

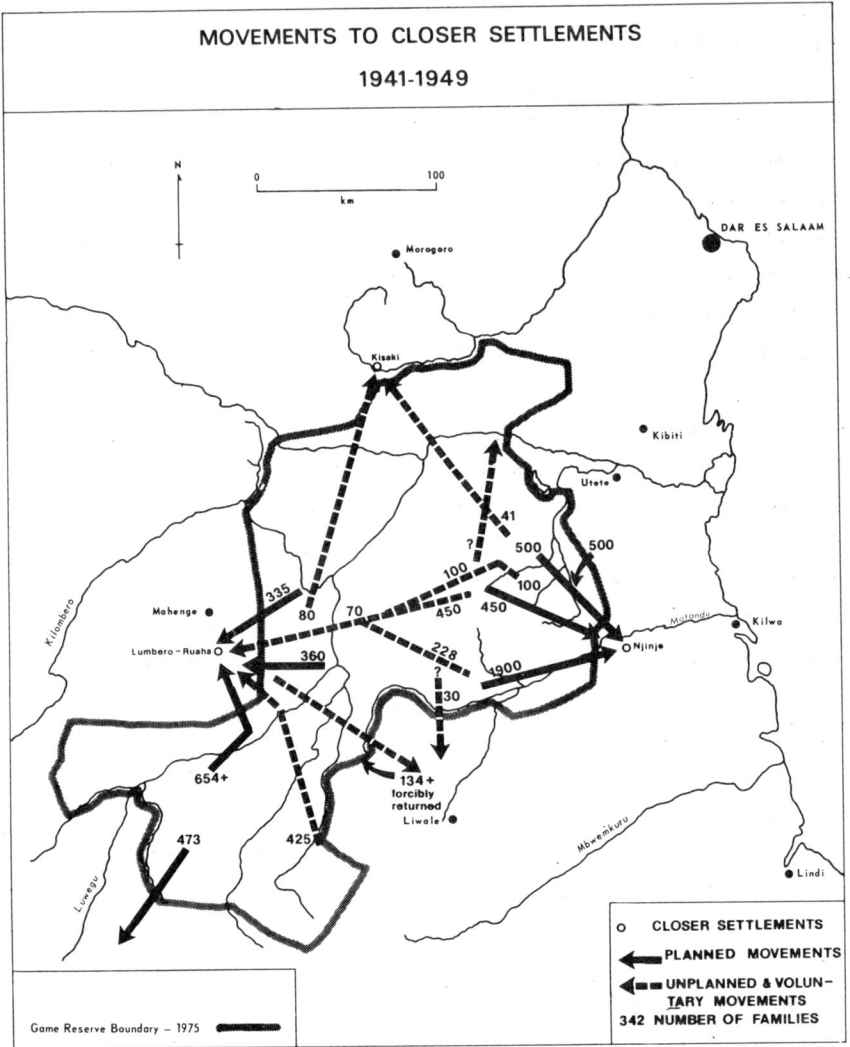

FIGURE 11

provided the impetus for an administrative decision to evacuate thousands of square miles of territory and to forbid its reoccupation. The expansion of the game reserve system assured that the resettlement prohibition was enforced. After independence, the game reserve started being viewed as an asset in its own right and additional pieces of territory were annexed to enhance wildlife values. Through the long history of its creation many forces were at work; nevertheless the result was usually the same--the Selous Game Reserve expanded as a wildlife sanctuary devoid of people.

Having examined the broad picture of change in southeastern Tanzania, the next chapter switches the level of resolution and examines a particular locality together with the people who have lived in it. The specific case is examined to demonstrate how the more general events discussed heretofore have impacted on a people and their wildlife environment.

Chapter II

THE MATANDU STUDY AREA AND ITS PEOPLE

The Selection of the Study Area

The Selous Game Reserve was much too large for the collection of field data for this study. In order to make the task more manageable, an area centered on the Matandu River was selected (Figure 12). The Matandu valley was particularly well suited for the study of human-wildlife interactions in woodland areas because of its physical characteristics, human history, lack of serious disturbance factors, and accessibility. Its salient features were:

1. substantial areas of miombo woodlands broken by a catena system of valleys containing open country. This is a common pattern throughout southeastern Tanzania.[1]
2. its numerous settlement sites abandoned during the 1940s' sleeping sickness evacuations.
3. its area of "virgin" country which was opened up to settlement in the 1950s. This provided several examples of village site selection in circumstances where no competition for land existed.
4. its settlement sites which were only recently (1969) abandoned.
5. the presence of traditional settlement just downstream outside of the game reserve. This provided a location for a case study of a village.
6. the numerous former inhabitants living near the reserve who were available for interviews.
7. its lack of illegal hunting activities which might have changed the animal behavior patterns. During the entire study period no sign of such hunting was encountered, although illegal fishing activities were frequently encountered.

---

[1] See Matzke, 1975, pp. 77-89 for details of vegetation and physical environment of the Matandu study area.

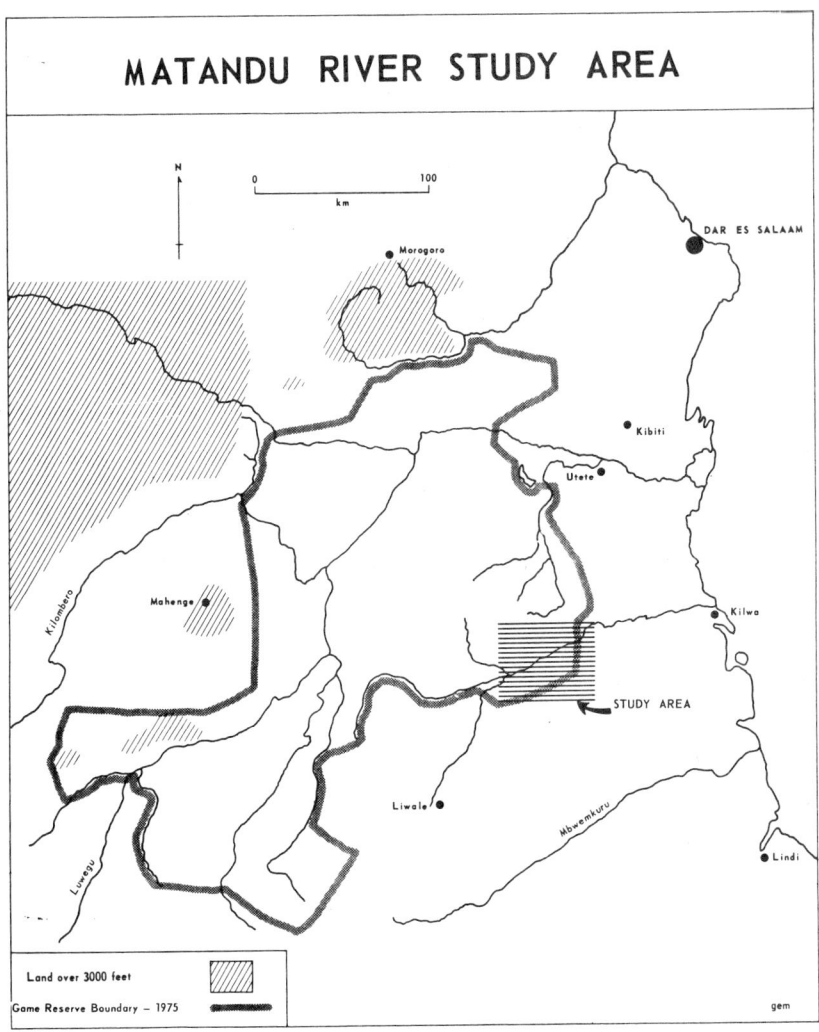

FIGURE 12

8. the absence of routes regularly traveled by humans which might add a serious disturbance factor. During the entire study period no vehicle other than the author's passed over many of the tracks.

9. the network of virtually unused, but serviceable, tracks to facilitate vehicular use in field study.

The Ngindo Inhabitants and the Location of Their Villages

The Matandu valley upstream from Njinjo is entirely within the locality traditionally claimed by the Ngindo people. These people, as was noted earlier, reacted to the relative peace and stability of the 20th century by descending from the thickets into valley bottom locations. Here they existed in long ribbon settlements with each family being out of sight of the next. Although their overall density in the area did not exceed about two people per square mile (.8 p. km^2), their actual density in the river valleys themselves was considerably higher. Counting only the space in the valley bottom itself, the density over the entire length of the Muhinje valley system was certainly over 40 per square mile (15 p. km^2) in 1945.

The Ngindo practiced a modified form of shifting cultivation. On the valley slopes, trees were cut and fields planted with crops such as sorghum, cassava, cow peas, and vegetables. These fields were regularly abandoned every few years as their fertility declined. The valley bottoms were much more fertile and the fields of rice and maize were rarely rested, if at all. The great majority of Ngindo completely abandoned their locations at irregular intervals and thereby changed the simple practice of shifting cultivation to something which might be termed "nomadic cultivation."

Table Two shows that twelve families interviewed for their history of relocations had moved an average of every 8-9 years to places far removed from their point of origin. In addition to this, they relocated at least once within the vicinity occupied after each major move. It is impossible to

TABLE TWO
RECORDS OF MAJOR RELOCATIONS IN THE LIVES OF SOME NGINDO PEOPLE WHO HAD FORMERLY LIVED IN THE SELOUS GAME RESERVE[1]

Name	Age (est.)	Number of Relocations	Involuntary Relocations[2]
Gabunda A.	60	5	2
Gabunda B.	50	4	2
Keusi A.	65	8	2
Keusi B.	75	10	2
Matule	60	6	2
Kujogopa A.	80	10	2
Kujogopa B.	70	9	2
Kichote	75	5	2
Ligogi	55	6	1
Mfaume	42	5	1
Mwechande	70	10	3
Mitondo	25	3	0*
Total	617	72	17

Average stay between major relocations was 8.57 years. (Standard Deviation is 2.45). Involuntary relocations represented 24% of the total.

[1] These records represent moves of distances in excess of 8 kilometers from the previous homestead. This record represents a minimum of moves by each individual since many interviewees failed to report visits with relatives or Dar es Salaam work periods which may have been several years in duration. In addition to these moves, people averaged one minor relocation at each place which necessitated building a new house.

[2] These were moves required by government as either a part of the sleeping sickness concentrations or the ujamaa village program.

*Taken from a record in the National Archives (44/2/37) recorded in 1933.

explain these moves on the basis of the depletion of soil fertility.

Carneiro (1956) has shown that tropical environments can sustain sedentary villages under conditions of shifting cultivation.[1] He suggested that if the "record reveals periodic relocations of villages of 500 persons or less, causes other than soil depletion should be assumed to have been responsible unless there is clear and conclusive evidence to the contrary." (p. 233)

It has already been shown that Ngindo did not live in agglomerations of 500 people. Most valleys contained fewer than 500 people unless they were of considerable length.[2] It remains a mystery why the people felt it necessary to move so often under conditions of low density. It was undoubtedly possible to exist quite well without moving and the few individuals who do so were praised by the colonial administration (44/2/57).

The Ngindo themselves give a wide range of explanations for their behavior. Occasionally they say that a particular move was prompted by agricultural concerns such as moving from a thicket to a valley where they could grow rice and sorghum. More often, however, they give reasons related to kinship responsibilities, minor conflicts with other people, or authority, or a general feeling that they were tired of the place and it was about time to move. Newman's (1969) discussion

---

[1] A check of a map shows Carneiro's Brazilian study area to be in a climate similar to that of Ngindoland. Nevertheless, he suggests that his findings should apply to the shifting cultivation practices of "primitive people in general" (p. 233).

[2] The headmen of Muhinje Juu and Muhinje Chini had a combined total of 670 families in 1945. This included the people of the valley and the hinterland as well. The headman at Mkondo in the Nkondaji valley had just over 1,000 families, but this total included people from as far away as the eastern side of the Tundu Hills.

of mobility among the Sandawe includes a good summary of motivations for moving that applies substantially to the Ngindo.[1]

Quite often a decision by one person sets off a veritable chain reaction of moves by other individuals. Junior relatives feel obligated to follow the lead of their elders and the abandonment of a valley by one group of people seems to create a feeling of insecurity in those remaining. The herd instinct takes over and the entire settlement location is abandoned within a period of a few years.

It is clear from the foregoing discussion that the Ngindo do not attach strong importance to a particular place. Rather, a nomad psychology prevails which keeps them circulating within the confines of Ngindoland and even beyond. This is not to imply that they will move anywhere; the constraints on the new locations are often socially determined. Thus, the spatial constraints to any move are not rigid in space over time. As a society changes with birth, marriages, deaths, and illnesses, so do the spatial options of any particular person seeking a new location. Soja's (1971) characterization of "a social definition of territory" seems appropriate in this situation. It is particularly useful to the Ngindo people whose circumstances have kept them continually ready to move. The settlement pattern reflected a people whose society was not rigidly defined in space.

When a group of people have a society which is defined territorially, the most likely place for the expansion of that territory is the settled fringe. In many places human settlement in newly opened lands expands along a frontier from the point of origin. The human encroachment of wildlife areas near Tsavo National Park in Kenya showed such a pattern (Capone, 1972). In the case of the Ngindo, the pattern is much different. The elimination of the Matandu Game Reserve opened the entire area

---

[1] The exceptions being that Ngindo have no livestock so they do not move to improve grazing. Likewise, there is no movement to mission stations since this is a Muslim area.

south of the Matandu River to settlement. Originally, people were confined to the easternmost section where they were located in sleeping sickness concentrations. Once the wholesale abandonment of these locations got underway, new settlements first sprung up some 45 miles (75 kilometres) away instead of on the fringes of the sleeping sickness settlements. (Figure 13)

The people in the villages of Lijungu and Ngambira skipped over many potential sites on the way to their chosen locations. Somewhat later, the site of Horowe, which was much closer to the sleeping sickness settlements, was occupied, but its first residents came there via an interim location at Narangombe some 45 miles (75 kilometres) from the sleeping sickness concentrations.

The twentieth century settlement history as far as is known to the author is summarized on Figure 13. In view of the Ngindos' nomadic instinct, the picture on the map conceals a great deal of instability. Settlements often were founded, expanded, contracted and completely abandoned while others persisted in spite of a considerable turnover of residents.

It is useful to consider the processes involved in the decision making for the selection of a new site. By so doing, one can better understand the resultant settlement pattern.

The villages throughout the Selous area were not randomly located with reference to the resource base needed to provide sustenance. In addition to physical resource pre-requisites, certain socially desirable requirements were weighed in the decision making of the village locators.

Chisholm (1968) saw five factors of importance in locating subsistence villages; they were: 1) Grazing land, 2) Water, 3) Building Materials, 4) Fuel, 5) Arable land. He called these the universal economic needs of an agricultural economy. The relative importance of these needs was shown by assigning each an index number according to its relative cost. For example, the frequency of use and difficulty of transport gave water an index of 10 while the spasmodic nature of the

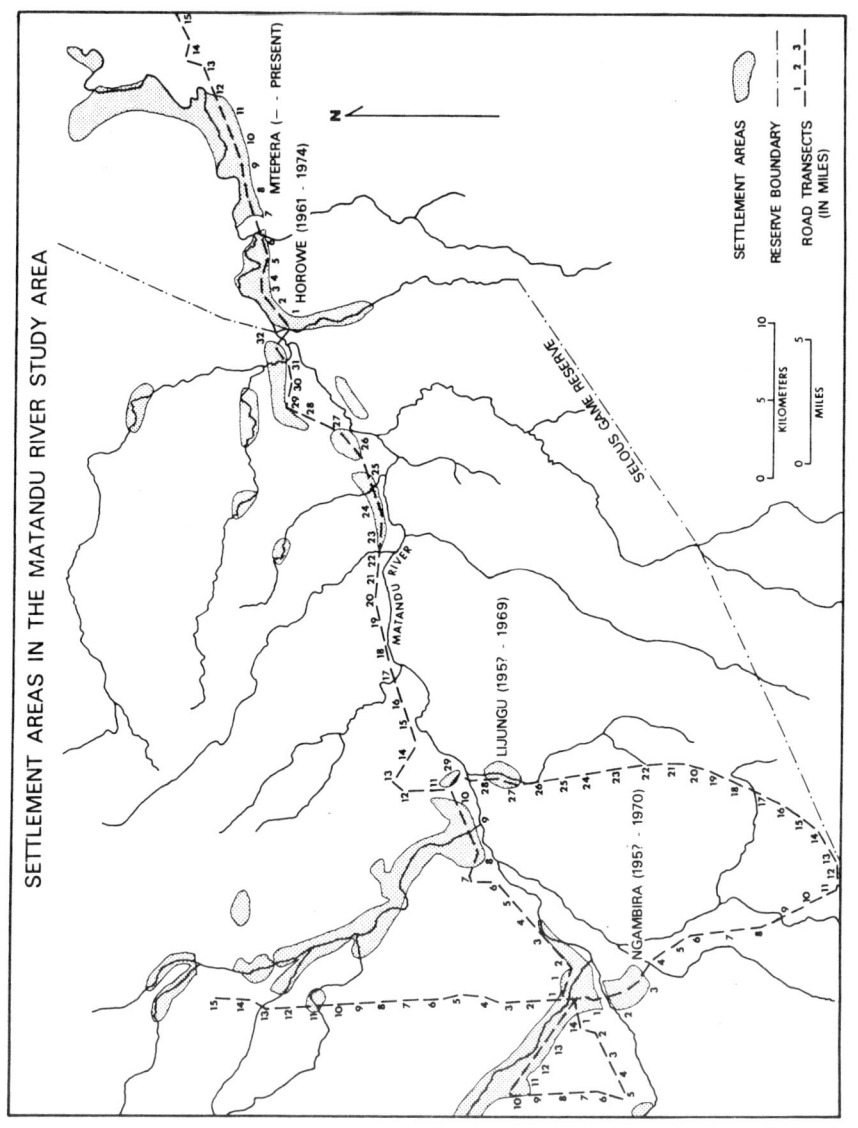

FIGURE 13

demand for building materials gave them an index number of 1. The most desirable site could be chosen by multiplying the distance each item was from the site by that item's index number and summing the results for each of the alternative sites. The one with the lowest total would be the logical choice for a village site.

An analysis such as that of Chisholm has only limited usefulness since it already assumes that the choices have somehow been narrowed to several select locations. In order to understand the process involved in site selection over an area with as many possibilities as the Selous, some additional conceptualization is necessary. It is suggested here that there are two major categories of factors influencing village site selection in conditions similar to those of the aboriginal Selous area. First, there is a set of macro-determinant items which will be weighed in order to select a particular river valley. Secondly, there is a set of micro-determinants which will affix within that river valley the exact location for the village in question. A useful categorization might be as follows:

Macro-determinants in Village Location
1. Social-spiritual constraints.
2. Permanent water.
3. Fertile soil.
4. Wildlife abundance.
5. Relative location of externalities.

Micro-determinants in Village Location
1. Social-spiritual constraints.
2. Edaphic physiography.
3. Security needs.
4. Firewood.
5. Building materials.

The distances separating villages in the study area were much greater than would have been necessitated by the available resource base alone. The Madaba locality, for example, had an area suitable for settlement that was eight miles long (Annual Reports, 1939). However, before it was selected as a place for a closer settlement, its small population never even approached full utilization of its arable land. As has already been noted, the social group preferences of the inhabitants were such that they preferred clan-sized agglomerations. Consequently, many villages were established long before older locations reached their maximum densities based on the human carrying capacity of the arable land.

Just as social considerations were of prime importance in spawning the need for a new village, they were of the first order of importance as a macro-determinant in selecting that village's location. For instance, a matter of prime importance would be the boundaries of the tribal area in question. Normally a move would not be made outside the area understood to be the domain of the Ngindo. Even within these areas, such places as were considered to be religiously taboo would be eliminated. A large forest section south of the Matandu River and the Kingombechimo area east of Madaba had special taboos that are still of concern today (Barongo, 1966).

The permanent water and fertile soil requirements are most likely to be found within river valleys for reasons previously discussed. Without these, the village cannot exist. However, a variety of locations fit the requirements of the first three "must have" macro-determinants. In order to further narrow the range of choices, the abundance of wildlife and the relative location of external places such as other villages with relatives, tax collectors, or shops are the final macro-determinants that select a particular valley location.

Once the valley is selected, the actual site selection is influenced by micro-determinant factors. First of all, religious and cultural taboos rule out certain areas. For instance, many people will not locate in the darkness of a forest, or near the site of a baobab tree (<u>Adansonia digitata</u> L.).[1] Next, the edaphic physiography is of importance since floods and malarial areas must be avoided.[2] Security needs are better met by an open ridge top site than in a thicket criss-crossed with elephant trails. After all of these things have been considered, a purely least cost Chisholmian economic analysis using firewood, building materials, etc. can be considered to have some bearing on the final site selection.

An understanding of the nature of the site selection considerations is vital to gaining a proper perspective of the role of the settled areas in limiting wildlife production. First, these considerations tended to maximize, rather than minimize the number of villages needed for a given number of people. Second, several of these considerations are identical to those which will make the sites chosen very essential to the wildlife in the area.

The Case Study of Horowe Village

The colonial government's attempt to concentrate people in Njinjo vicinity was successful only in the short run. Immediately upon their arrival, the Ngindo started to agitate for permission to leave and resettle elsewhere. By 1947, they had started to resettle the Ngarambi area across from the present site of the Miombo Research Centre. Although this was initially resisted by colonial authorities,[3] the persistence of the Ngindo

---

[1] A taboo against cutting down baobab trees exists amongst the Ngindo. This was discovered when I attempted to hire men to cut one down during the construction of an airstrip.

[2] The Ngindo have a set of vegetative indicators of suitable physiographic conditions. A discussion and partial listing of these is included in Appendix C of Matzke, 1975.

[3] See, for instance, the letter from the Provincial Commissioner of the Southern Province to the District Commissioner of Kilwa dated Feb. 1, 1947. He (P.C.) orders the D.C. to send out a patrol to destroy the homes of people who have gone back to Ngarambi and either send them away or prosecute them (19/79).

prevailed. Over the next decade a diaspora was in the making as people left the concentrations and pioneered settlement along the borders of the game reserve. It was during this time that the villages of Lijungu, Ngambira, and Horowe were established. These villages were nestled along the south side of the Matandu River which was then the border of the reserve.

Each of these villages took its name from the small tributary valley along which the scattered sorghum fields were located. Following the traditional pattern of a broken ribbon string of cultivation, these villages with less than a few hundred people each were dispersed over the countryside for a distance of up to 10 miles.

The extension of the game reserve boundaries had eliminated Ngambira and Lijungu settlements by the time this study was undertaken. Only Horowe was left with inhabitants for the author to interview, so it was chosen for closer examination. Unfortunately, a program of resettlement into <u>Ujamaa</u> villages eliminated Horowe in September 1974 before all of the interviews were completed, but sufficient information was obtained to give an outline of the growth and death of this village.

In about 1961, three different heads of families made apparently independent decisions to locate in the Horowe River valley eight miles west of the nearest settlement of Mtepera on the Matandu River. All three of these men were over 50 years old at the time and had formerly lived in the game reserve. The decision of these three men had a bandwagon effect as their younger brothers, other relatives, and even strangers soon followed. By 1966, the settlement extended four miles up the Horowe River and four miles downstream along the Matandu (Figure 13). At the time of its maximum extent, it probably contained no more than 150 families.

The narrow flood plain of the Matandu River provided a bit of acreage which was devoted to rice and maize farming, but the mainstay of the people was sorghum. The slightly elevated lands along the Matandu and the entire Horowe valley were favorable for the production of this stable crop. The unpredictability of the rains, and the uncertainty of flooding, made the production of rice an especially risky proposition.

The pioneer settlers claim that the locality they selected was filled with animals when they first arrived. They specifically mention wildebeest, impala, hartebeest, waterbuck, and eland as having been present; buffalo and sable were especially plentiful.[1] Initially, these animals caused considerable damage to crops, but this lessened with time and only the elephant remained as a large and consistent trouble maker. The villagers universally attribute the observed reduction of the animal population to the activities of humans. As evidence, they point to the animals which can be found a short distance away in the uninhabited game reserve.

The presence of the game reserve was a mixed blessing. Initially, it was only a game controlled area where hunting was forbidden, but honey gathering continued. Illegal hunting was undertaken regularly, but became exceedingly risky as the game reserve boundaries were extended to the north side of the Matandu within a mile of the village in 1964. A number of the villagers were arrested for poaching as game scout patrols were stepped up in the area. In 1970, the game reserve boundary was extended up the Horowe River and the farmers in the Horowe valley abandoned their locations. This marked the start of a decline in population which culminated with the last villager being removed to an _ujamaa_ village on September 29, 1974.

With the disappearance of people from the Matandu valley, one important active element in the ecosystem was removed. The daily presence of settlement and its associated activities no longer influenced the physical and biological environment.

The foregoing discussion has sketched a basic outline of the human components of the Matandu study site. Chapter Three will add another dimension with the introduction of large

---

[1] See Appendix A for the Latin binomials of all animals mentioned in this work.

mammals into the system. The large mammal populations are especially important because concern for their well-being is an important force keeping human settlement at bay. It is assumed that the presence of humans is detrimental to their survival. If this is true, so is the converse: the absence of humans is beneficial. The investigation of the large mammal populations is aimed at illuminating the links between the human and wildlife populations which have coexisted in the Matandu Valley.

Chapter III

THE WILDLIFE SCENE

The Wildlife Picture in the Past

The wildlife picture in the past only can be sketched in its barest outlines from early explorers reports and the memories of early inhabitants. The sources often are contradictory and subject to considerable bias. There are no data available from actual field counts anywhere in the Selous until the establishment of the Miombo Research Centre in 1968. In the country around the research center there is evidence to show that the numbers of waterbuck, impala, and wildebeest have been increasing (Rodgers, 1969). What cannot be said, however, is what caused their previous lower populations.

Nicholson (1969) is of the opinion that the present day Selous Game Reserve has "a game population many times greater than it was when the first Europeans penetrated the country." To this he adds that "in 1948, when the last of the people were evacuated, the game population was at an all time low." The record as I have been able to piece it together lends some support to his second contention with reference to particular species.[1] It definitely does not support this assertion for other species, most notably elephant.

The early European reports indicate in a general way that large mammals were common in the parklands north of the Rufiji River. Both Speke (1864) and Thomson (1968) mention seeing and hunting "antelopes" there. The locations they traversed were not in miombo, but rather the dry open plains which today contain heavy densities of plains game. Settlements occurred only on the edges of these expanses along the Rufiji, BehoBeho, and Mgeta Rivers.

---

[1] S. Marks (pers. Comm.) has suggested low numbers could be the result of a rinderpest epidemic. B. Nicholson (pers. comm.) says that the epidemic did not enter Selous.

The only early records from the miombo of the Selous are contained in Thomson's account of his crossing the Selous' northeastern corner (this section was ceded to Mikumi National Park in 1974). He remarked,

> In few parts of the world, with everything apparently favorable for the rearing of abundant animal life, is there such a marked absence of it without an assignable cause. (Thomson, 1968, p. 173)

He was making his traverse just after the completion of the rains and before the passing of the fire. Even today, the long grasses of the miombo are not attractive to much wildlife at that time of the year. From the tracks he saw he confirmed that the area contained "elephant, buffalo, antelope, and quagga (zebra)."

The next records from the Selous miombo come from Sutherland (1912) who spent six years hunting elephants in southern Tanzania. From the Mbarangandu and Njenje Rivers he recorded:

> after several days of promiscuous hunting I had managed to get several fine heads including sable and roan antelopes, a leopard, an eland and one or two antelopes.

Since roan antelope do not occur in this area (Dorst and Dadelot, 1970), the quality of his observations is suspect. Nevertheless it seems clear that his main quarry, elephant, was abundant. Among many others, he records shooting three elephants with ivory over 100 lbs. per tusk with the biggest (152 lbs.) taken on the Njenje River.

The records of an abundance of elephants in the miombo traversed by Sutherland coincide with game preservation department reports of their abundance in the game reserve north of the Rufiji. In sharp contrast to this is the unanimous opinion of those interviewed who lived to the south and east of the Rufiji River. The accounts of these people tell of the near elephant free existence which they lived until the "Government of the English" arrived. In addition to the interviews conducted for this study, both Rodgers (pers. comm.) and Crosse-Upcott (1956) have noted the alleged invasion of elephants. The story is often embellished with a detailed explanation of the route taken by the elephants as they invaded from Ulanga to the west.

It would be easy to dismiss this story as one that has been retold so often that even the tellers started believing it. From the evidence that is now available, an alternative explanation is possible.

The ivory trade in Africa had been intensively exploiting the elephant populations since the 16th century. According to Spinage (1973) it collapsed after overexploitation between 1840-1890. Kilwa was a major center for the exportation of ivory and a number of caravan routes went through the vicinity of the study area. It is quite probable that the elephants there suffered disproportionately from the demands for ivory. Thomson remarked that in 1878 "evil days had befallen the elephant... and now not one is to be seen in the jungles which surround Mahenge." (p. 177) The survivors must certainly have done their best to avoid human habitation.

The coming of colonial rule changed the situation. "Subsequent protection has apparently enabled surviving elephants to enter an exponential phase of population increase." (Spinage, 1973, p. 287)

During World War I, heavy shooting in Portuguese East Africa forced large numbers of elephants north into southern Tanzania (22/17). The elephant population had increased considerably by the 1930s if one is to judge by the reports of crop damage in the colonial records for the Southern Province. In response to this, a large elephant control operation was mounted in the Kilwa hinterlands (Table Three) and many herds moved west into the Selous. In addition, the Mtetesi Game Reserve was eliminated and the elephants were forced out of that location.

The arrival of large numbers of strange elephants coincided with the implementation of a policy of selective protection of big villages. The Ngindo were particularly vulnerable. The cultivation protector observed:

There are about 2 natives to one square mile, and one elephant to every four natives, and natives are spread all over the district in the smallest communities of 3 to 10 huts, and on the other hand elephants are raiding in herds of 50 to 100 (22/3)

TABLE THREE

ELEPHANTS SHOT FOR CULTIVATION PROTECTION IN THE SOUTHERN PROVINCE

Year	Elephant Numbers	Ivory lbs.	Kgs.
1931	350	12,382	5,628
1932	399	14,284	6,493
	Start of Kilwa Control Scheme		
1933	764	25,319	11,509
1934	1,165	31,367	14,258
1935	1,796	37,600	17,100

From the sequence of events thus portrayed, it is quite possible that the local inhabitants' accounts of an elephant invasion is based on a real happening. The populations which were recovering from a period of overexploitation were swelled by the migration of large numbers from Mozambique and control schemes in the Southern Province. When the protection of game staff was denied, people experienced greatly increased losses to elephants. They reacted accordingly:

> They have an elephant complex, it is a case of elephant here, elephant there, elephant almost everywhere and live largely in the shambas (fields) to scare off the elephant. (19/75)

It seems clear from the above that the elephant populations were on the increase before the removal of people. The establishment of the game reserve and the removal of settlement probably accelerated the growth of the elephant population as it became an even more attractive haven from harassment and human induced mortality.

The documentary evidence for the abundance of species other than elephants is scarce. The early Europeans were not trained naturalists so their records group everything together into the category of "antelope" except for buffalo, zebra and elephants. The first record with more specific names comes from Sutherland. He was followed by several of the combatants from World War I who shot wildebeest, hippo, elephant, and sable. Lettow-Vorbeck (1957) reported that game abounded in the parkland areas around Lake Utungi, but mentions nothing of the miombo areas further to the west. Because of the paucity of written sources, it was necessary to turn to the memories of the former inhabitants as the sole source of information on the abundance and distribution of game during times past.

Tape recorded interviews were held with former inhabitants and among other things they were asked to recall as best they could the animals which had been present in the vicinity of villages where they had formerly lived in the game reserve. Likewise, they were asked to indicate which animals were definitely not present during their tenure there. The data thus obtained are summarized in Table Four.

The standard with which to compare people's recollections of the past is the present. Two measures of perceived animal abundance, the frequency of sightings and the total number of animals seen, are given in Table Five. Along with these measures is reported the average herd size which explains the relationship between the two. These data are from transect counts undertaken in the game reserve portion of the study area. They give the reader a feel for how often he would encounter the different species if he passed through at the present time. If one so desired, he could easily change the frequency of encounter by being selective in the habitats traversed. Nevertheless, for the nonsecretive species utilizing the major

TABLE FOUR

INTERVIEWEE RESPONSES TO THE FORMER OCCURRENCE OF SELECTED ANIMALS[1]

Species	Locations % Present	Locations % Absent	N
1. Sable	100		7
2. Kudu	100		6
3. Eland	100		5
4. Hartebeest	100		5
5. Duiker	100		4
6. Bushbuck	100		3
7. Reedbuck	75*	25	4
8. Zebra	50*	50	4
9. Wildebeest	40**	60	5
10. Impala	20	80	5
11. Waterbuck	17	83	6
12. Buffalo	12	86	8

*Each asterisk indicates a response that was qualified by an addition that there very few of this particular animal present.

[1] The data presented here were gleaned from tape recorded conservations with a number of former residents of the Selous Game Reserve. People representing 10 former village locations in miombo areas were included. They were asked to describe the animals which they remembered as having been present or absent from the vicinity of their previous residences. No checklist was given them so many animals were just not mentioned. Although it often represents the effort of many individuals, each village location was only recorded once for each species. Only animals mentioned in reference to at least 3 villages were included. Elephant are treated separately because an apparent sharp increase in numbers during the 1930s resulted in answers being qualified in time.

TABLE FIVE

RANK ORDER OF TOTAL SIGHTINGS, NUMBERS, AND AVERAGE HERD SIZE

	Number of Animals Seen			Number of Sightings			Average Herd Size	
1.	Impala	8284	1.	Hartebeest	875	1.	Buffalo	107.2
2.	Buffalo	4610	2.	Impala	755	2.	Wildebeest	11.8
3.	Wildebeest	3824	3.	Warthog	492	3.	Impala	11.0
4.	Hartebeest	3771	4.	Wildebeest	323	4.	Eland	10.3
5.	Zebra	1429	5.	Elephant	274	5.	Zebra	6.3
6.	Waterbuck	1118	6.	Duiker	240	6.	Sable	5.5
7.	Warthog	1107	7.	Zebra	227	7.	Waterbuck	5.1
8.	Elephant	1034	8.	Waterbuck	218	8.	Bushpigs	5.
9.	Eland	780	9.	Reedbuck	128	9.	Hartebeest	4.3
10.	Reedbuck	320	10.	Eland	76	10.	Elephant	3.8
11.	Duiker	244	11.	Buffalo	43	11.	Wild Dogs	3.5
12.	Kudu	122	12.	Kudu	41	12.	Kudu	3.0
13.	Sable	53	13.	Oribi	15	13.	Reedbuck	2.5
14.	Oribi	23	14.	Lion	8	14.	Warthog	2.3
15.	Bushbuck	13	15.	Bushbuck	7	15.	Bushbuck	1.9
16.	Lion	10	16.	Sable	6	16.	Oribi	1.5
17.	Wild Dogs	7	17.	Hyena	3	17.	Lion	1.3
18.	Bushpigs	5	18.	Wild Dogs	2	18.	Duiker	1.0
19.	Hyena	3	19.	Rhino	1	19.	Hyena	1
20.	Rhino	1	20.	Leopard	1	20.	Rhino	1
	Leopard	1		Jackal	1		Jackal	1
	Jackal	1		Bushpig	1		Leopard	1

These data are the totals for all animals, except Hippo, which were recorded during a total of 23 repetitions of the transects inside the Selous Game Reserve. This includes a total of 2,111.4 linear miles of observations. Because of considerably different conditions on the transect outside the reserve, the animals sighted thereon are not included in the above totals.

habitat types, it is a reasonable approximation of how commonly they are seen.[1] Table Six selects the 12 species reported on by former residents and compares their former occurrence with the frequency of encounter of these same species in the present time. The categorization in Table Seven takes into account both the absolute number of animals seen and the number of animal groups sighted in assigning a species to a frequency of encounter category.

The striking thing to be observed in Table Six is that the animals now only rarely or infrequently seen (reedbuck, sable, bushbuck, kudu) were almost universally reported to be present in the past. On the other hand, all of the species reported to have been absent from 50% or more of the village sites reported on by the interviewees are now either common or very common. Even given that the data on the past situation are subject to many sources of error,[2] the gross pattern is difficult to ignore. For example, is it conceivable that one could deny the presence of buffalo (reported in only 1 of 8 villages) which is so destructive to life and property, while remembering the flighty sable antelope which never occurs in high densities and is harmless under most circumstances?

The data presented in Table Six raise questions with regard to particular species. The species can be grouped according to the common nature of the questions they raise.

<u>Group One</u>: Hartebeest, Eland, Duiker

These three species were reported in the vicinity of 100% of the villages. Since all of these species are commonly

---

[1] It should be noted that this is not the same as real density. Density can only be computed after adjusting for visibility and ensuring representative sampling procedures for all vegetation types.

[2] These include the small size of the sample, the selectivity of people's memory, and the varying degrees of importance placed on different animals by a person's cultural baggage.

TABLE SIX

FREQUENCY OF ENCOUNTER WITH 12 UNGULATE SPECIES IN THE SELOUS GAME RESERVE PORTION OF THE MATANDU STUDY AREA IN COMPARISON WITH REPORTS OF FORMER INHABITANTS

Frequency of encounter during transect counts[1]	% of villages reported to have species in vicinity by former residents[2]
Very Common[3]	
Impala	20%
Buffalo	12%
Wildebeest	40%
Hartebeest	100%
Common[4]	
Zebra	50%
Waterbuck	17%
Eland	100%
Duiker	100%
Infrequent[5]	
Reedbuck	75%
Kudu	100%
Rare[6]	
Sable	100%
Bushbuck	100%

[1] Constructed from data reported in Appendix B.

[2] From data reported in Table Four.

[3] An average of at least 1.5 animals seen per transect mile, or at least an average of one sighting every three miles.

[4] An average of between .25 and 1.5 animals per transect mile, or an average of one sighting for every 3 to 10 miles.

[5] An average of between .10 and .25 animals per transect mile, or an average of one sighting for every 10 to 200 miles.

[6] Requires an average of over 200 transect miles per sighting.

In order to examine the possible relationships between the former distribution of settlement and the former distribution of wildlife, it is necessary to make a close examination of the present distribution of wildlife with reference to old settlement sites. With this as background, it might be possible to assess any changes which might have occurred since the removal of people.

The Methodology of the Wildlife Census

The determination of the wildlife history in the Selous necessarily rests on the reports of others. This is not without its problems. An assessment of the current wildlife situation also presents problems, although of a different nature. Fortunately a growing body of literature is available to offer guidance. Of primary importance is that dealing with methods of estimating wildlife numbers.

The assessment of the current status of wildlife was aimed at providing the following information which is listed in the descending order of importance:

1. The correlation of animal distribution patterns to the location of village sites.
2. The seasonal changes in these distribution patterns.
3. The population size of each major species in the study area.
4. The habitats utilized by each species.

The priorities established here helped to eliminate some methodologies because they were not suited to providing good spatial correlations to particular sites (even though they were possibly superior for the estimation of population sizes e.g. random block censusing). A transect census methodology was modified for use in this research. A detailed description of its theory and application is given in Matzke (1976a).

encountered even today, their former occurrence is not surprising.

Group Two: Bushbuck, Reedbuck, Waterbuck

These three species pose serious methodological problems. In the case of waterbuck, the habitat requirements (surface water and associated vegetation) are so narrow that only a few areas along the major watercourses are really suitable for its maintenance. Few village sites met these requirements so their general absence in the past is not surprising. Reedbuck and bushbuck, on the other hand, occur in long grass and thicket vegetation where visibility is very poor. They appear infrequently in the transect counts for that reason. They are commonly found in places under cultivation and thus are more likely to be seen by a farmer on foot than by men passing along a transect in a Land Rover. The methodology of the transect count, in the absence of a correction for visibility, thus grossly under represents their current abundance.

Group Three: Sable, Kudu

These two species are relatively uncommon in the study area today. Without exception, however, they were reported as being present in the locations cited by former residents. In view of the fact that many of the common species were reported as being absent, one asks why these two species were recorded as being present.

Group Four: Impala, Buffalo, Wildebeest, Zebra

These four species are common today, but were recorded as not present in at least half of the villages reported on by the interviewees. These animals raise the most interesting questions. By the measures of frequency used here, one would expect that any resident would encounter all of these species with considerable regularity. Since they so often were reported absent, is it possible to assume their former abundance was but a fraction of their current numbers?

Wildlife Patterns in the Study Area

The wildlife census was undertaken over a period of one complete year in order to observe the changes which occurred in distribution as the supporting resources fluctuated in both time and space. It was originally suggested that human settlement occupied critical resource areas. If the population of any species was found to be seasonally concentrated in a limited space, the denial of that space, and the resources contained therein, would have detrimental consequences for the population in question.

The fluctuation of the resource base was very much influenced by the passing of the seasons. Therefore, the data were gathered during three distinct seasons listed below:

1. <u>Early Dry Season</u>. This time period commenced when the grasses had sufficiently dried out to sustain burning. Except for waterlogged areas, green grass was rare. Surface water was widespread with the seasonal catchments drying out only near the end of the period. Fires were burning somewhere nearly every day. The landscape was a mosaic of brown grass and burned areas with occasional green patches around surface water supplies. These general conditions prevailed through August and September. The census period for this season was from September 9 through September 19, 1974.

2. <u>Late Dry Season</u>. The perennial grasses of the woodland areas started sprouting a few weeks after they were burned, or after receiving a substantial rainfall. By October, the woodlands had large areas in flush as the result of the fires. In the absence of any rains, these flushes died back while places which were fired at a later time started greening. At any one time, there was a patchwork pattern of unburned grass, burned areas with new grass, and burned areas with no grass. During this time, surface water became increasingly scarce and the patches of green grass associated with them grew smaller. The grasses of the seasonally flooded areas which retarded earlier

fires were themselves flammable in the late dry season. The census for this season took place from October 1973 through January 1974.

3. <u>Wet Season</u>. The wet season was defined by the coming of the rains which sustained the growth of grass to its mature height. Given the variability of the rains, this season may come as early as November or as late as March. It had definitely arrived by the end of February of 1974. With its arrival, water was universally available. Grasses were in excess of three feet high in most places. Short grass communities were in every case located along the drainage lines in the study area. The census for the wet season was undertaken between March 2 and June 15, 1974.

The census results give a clear indication that some species of ungulates in the study area responded to periodic changes in the resource base by moving to habitat types which presumably contained the resources most favorable to their support. The most striking examples of a seasonal shift were noted when the data were sorted according to the three seasons mentioned above and then further subdivided according to the four vegetation forms used in recording animal sightings along the transect routes. Some species showed a marked preference for particular vegetation types and that preference remained essentially unaltered year around. Other species showed considerable seasonal differences in the type of vegetation that they preferred.

Kudu, hartebeest and duiker are all essentially woodland animals. Their densities in the woodland portions of the transects (58% of total length) equalled, or exceeded the average density over the entire transect length including all vegetation types (Figures 14, 15, 16). Since nearly 60% of the study area was covered by woodland, the species utilizing the woodland had much space available for dispersal at all times of the year. The seasonal fluctuations in rainfall apparently did not

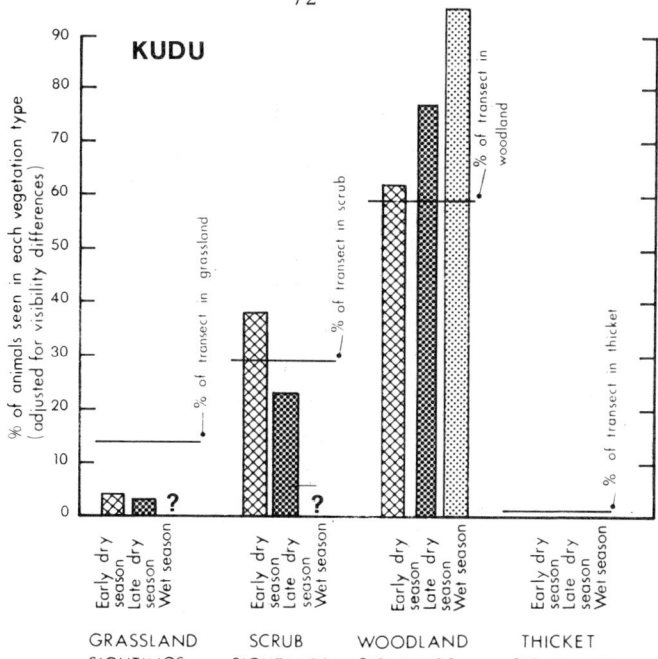

Figure 14   Kudu seasonal occurrence in four vegetation forms.

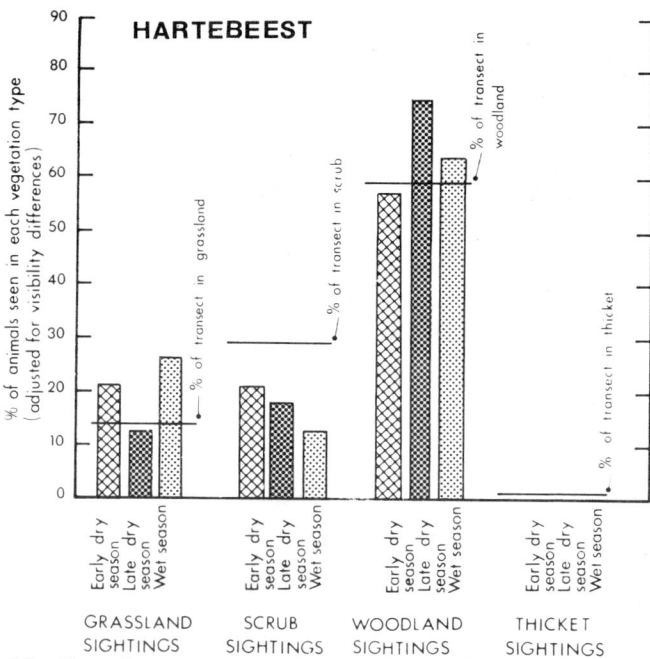

Figure 15   Hartebeest seasonal occurrence in four vegetation forms.

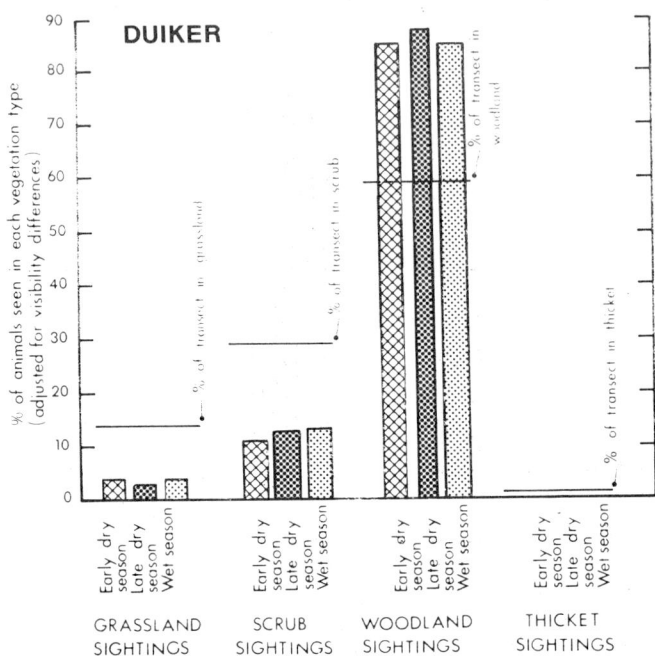

Figure 16 Duiker seasonal occurrence in four vegetation forms.

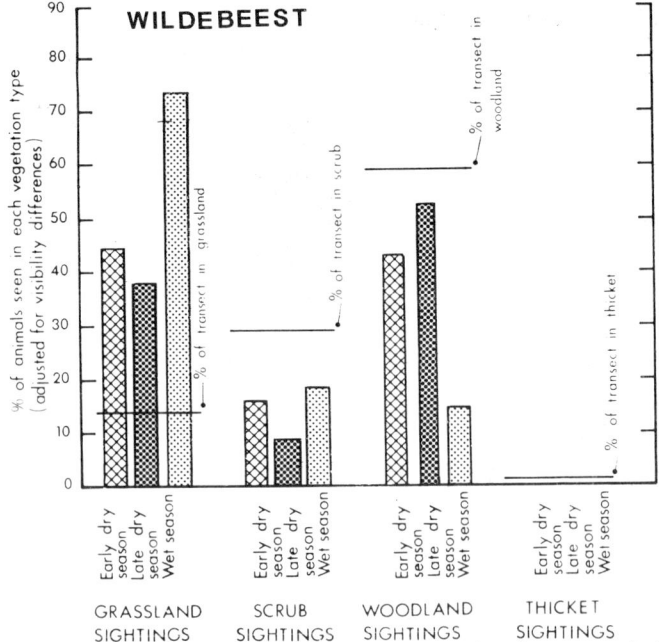

Figure 17 Wildebeest seasonal occurrence in four vegetation forms.

necessitate a marked migration from the woodland habitat in search of supportive resources. Although in one case, hartebeest, the grasslands actually supported higher densities than the woodlands, the total number of individuals occupying the grasslands never exceeded about one-quarter of the total sampled population. It is thought that the highly dispersed nature of the kudu, duiker, and hartebeest populations make them less likely to be seriously disturbed by the presence of isolated cultivators than would be the case for species whose individuals show marked concentrations of numbers in spatially restricted localities.

Wildebeest, impala, and warthog[1] all had at least 60 per cent of the individuals concentrated in the 13 per cent of the transect which was grassland during one, or more, seasons of the year (Figures 16, 17, 18). Wildebeest and impala were extremely mobile in their response to changing environmental conditions. When the fires had passed and the grasses of the woodland flushed, over half of the sampled individuals were found in the woodland. When the rains arrived and the length of the woodland grasses was above the desired height, most of the animals were found concentrated in the spatially restricted short grassland areas along drainage areas. In the case of wildebeest, the densities in these areas were 25 times the densities of the woodlands. (see Table Seven for all density figures.)

One measure of the degree of spatial restriction exhibited during the rainy season in shown in Figure 20. The cumulative percentage of the total individuals counted during the wet season is plotted against the transect miles which are rank ordered according to the number of individuals counted per mile. This

---

[1]The case of warthog (Figure 19) is not altogether clear because of the difficulty in seeing these animals in the long grasses found in the woodland during the rainy season. The author is not at all certain that the rainy season data are a reflection of the true picture. It is more likely that these data reflect a very high proportion of missed sightings close to the road in the woodland areas. The short grasslands therefore appear more important than they are in reality.

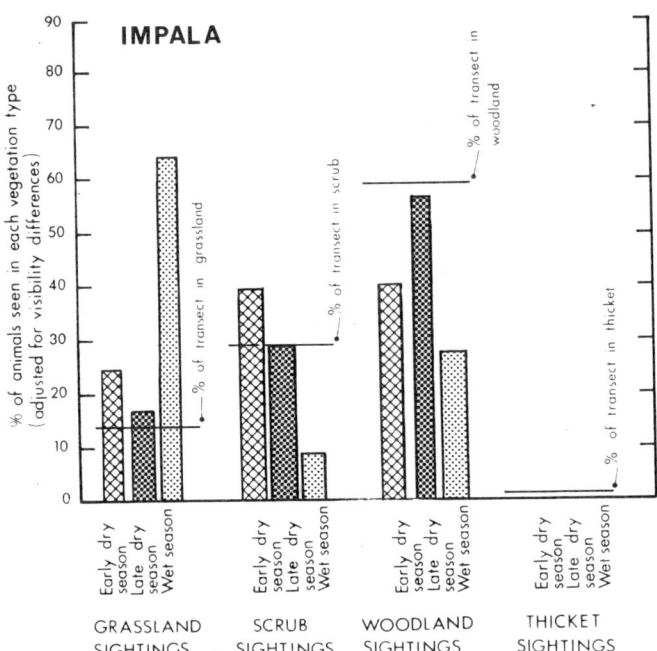

Figure 18 Impala seasonal occurrence in four vegetation forms.

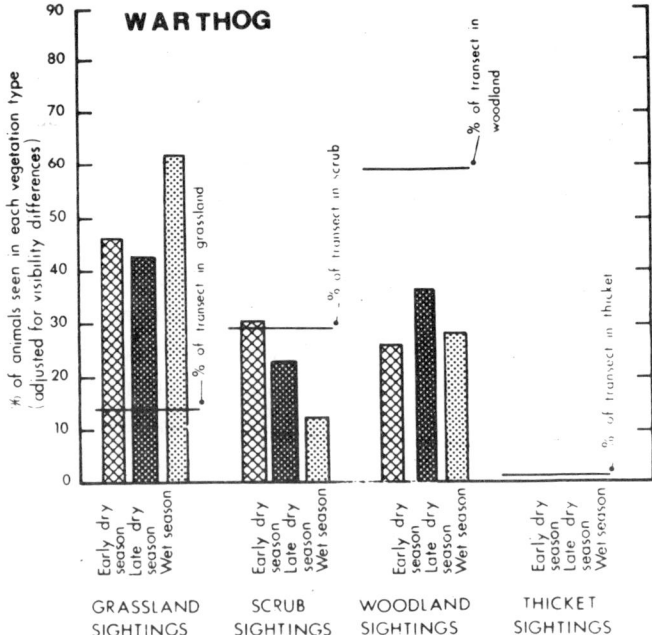

Figure 19 Warthog seasonal occurrence in four vegetation forms.

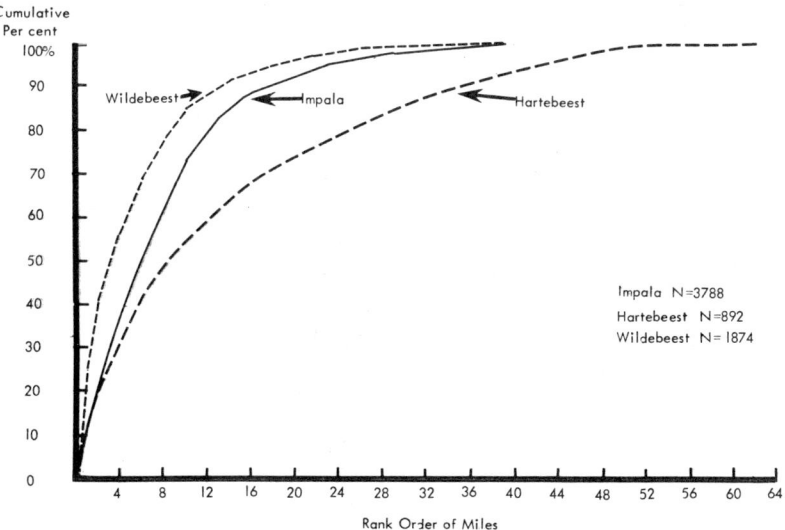

Figure 20 The spatial restriction of wildebeest, impala and hartebeest. Hartebeest with the fewest number of individuals were much more widespread during the rainy season than were wildebeest and impala.

shows that 75% of the individuals were counted in only five miles for wildebeest, 11 miles for impala, while it took 22 miles to count 75% of the hartebeest. Moreover, hartebeest, with less than one-half the numbers of wildebeest and one-quarter that of impala, were seen in two-thirds of the transect miles, while the other species were seen in only two-fifths of the possible miles.[1]

The situation for zebra and elephant is illustrated in Figures 21 and 22. It shows a buildup of numbers in the grasslands during the rainy season, but it is less marked than it was for wildebeest, impala and warthog. These intermediate cases had a half, or more, of their numbers in other habitat types year around. Their distributions were somewhat less restricted than either impala or wildebeest, but not as dispersed as hartebeest and duiker.

---

[1] There was a total of 91.8 miles traversed within the game reserve. These data are the totals for eight replicate counts of these miles.

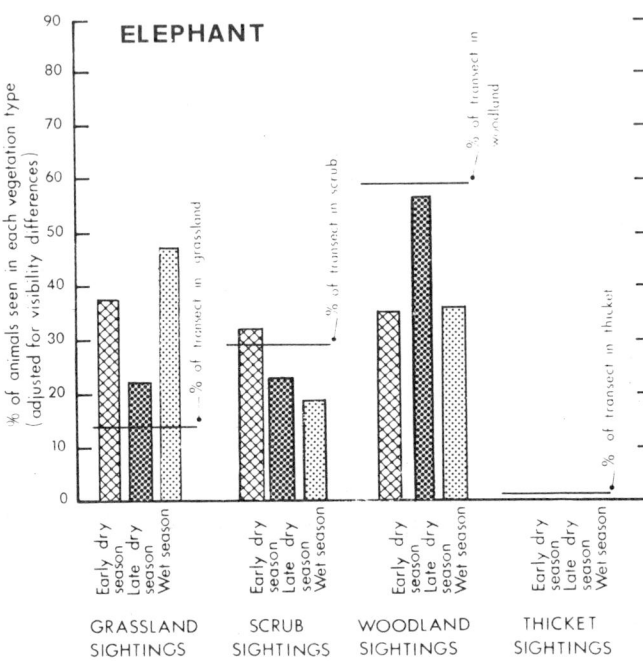

Figure 21 Elephant seasonal occurrence in four vegetation forms.

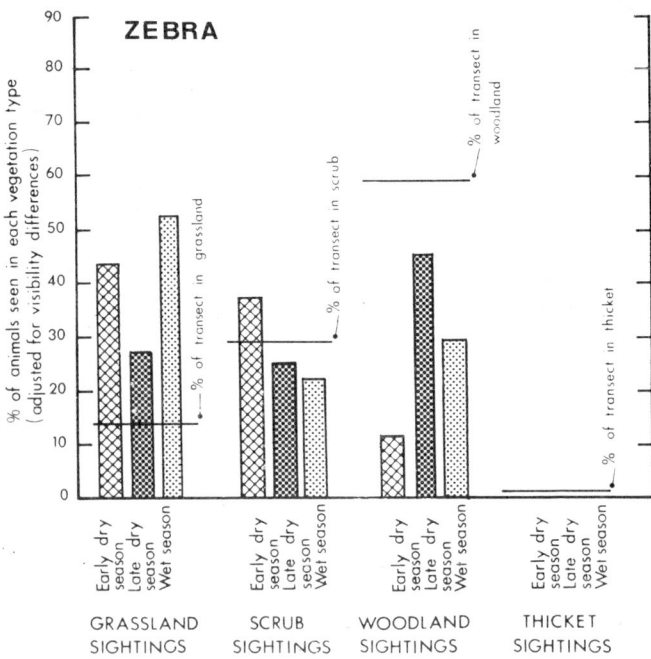

Figure 22 Zebra seasonal occurrence in four vegetation forms.

The elephant's ability to utilize a wider range of foods than the zebra probably accounts for its slightly more dispersed distribution during the rains. The utilization of long grass woodland and seasonally flooded habitats presents few obstacles for elephant. This is not the case with zebra. Figure 23 illustrates the differences in the degree of concentration between these two species; the zebra tends more toward the pattern set by wildebeest and impala while the elephant with much smaller numbers tends toward that of the hartebeest. (Refer to Figure 20.)

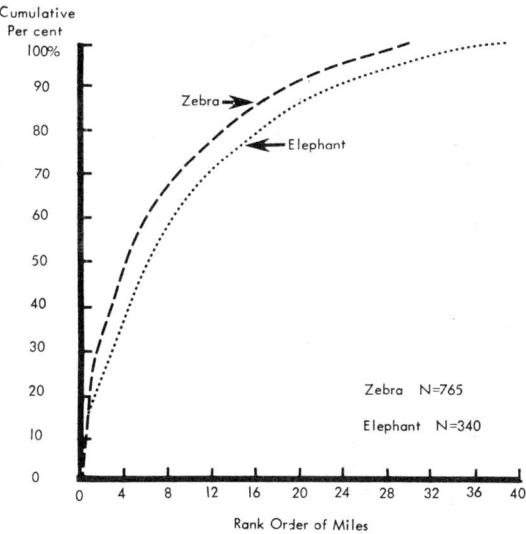

Figure 23 A comparison of the degree of dispersion shown by zebra and elephant.

Using the method of calculation discussed by Matzke (1976a), densities were computed for all species seen often enough to provide a data base for calculations. These densities are summarized in Table Seven. It is felt by the author that only impala, hartebeest, elephant, wildebeest, zebra, warthog, and possibly waterbuck met closely enough the conditions necessary for the application of the method. The data for the other

TABLE SEVEN

COMPUTED DENSITIES PER SQUARE MILE FOR ALL SPECIES, SEASONS AND VEGETATION TYPES

SPECIES	Early Dry Season				Late Dry Season				Wet Season				Combined
	$\bar{D}$	D_g	D_s	D_w	$\bar{D}$	D_g	D_s	D_w	$\bar{D}$	D_g	D_s	D_w	$\bar{D}_c$
Elephant	1.1	3.1	1.3	0.6	1.7	2.0*	1.3*	1.8	1.0	3.4	1.1	0.7	
Hartebeest	8.0	14.3	5.7	7.9	8.1	4.7	4.6	12.1	5.1	9.9	2.7	6.2	
Impala	13.3	28.2	17.9	8.3	14.0	15.7	14.0	15.1	19.8	94.1	7.1	9.1	
Warthog	3.9	13.4	4.3	2.0	3.7	12.5	3.6	1.8	1.1	4.4	0.3*	0.5*	
Waterbuck	1.9	3.8	5.7	1.0*	1.9	3.3	2.8	1.6	1.9	7.9*	1.5*	1.0*	
Wildebeest	4.4	14.0	2.1*	4.4	2.9	9.2	0.7*	2.4	6.5	36.5	3.2*	1.3	
Zebra	1.4	4.2	2.3*	0.1*	1.7	3.1	1.6*	1.3	2.8	12.2	1.6*	1.2	
	D				D				D				
Buffalo	12.2*	-	-	-	5.7*	-	-	-	2.3*	-	-	-	
Bushbuck	-	-	-	-	-	-	-	-	-	-	-	-	
Duiker	2.1	-	-	-	x	-	-	-	0.9	-	-	-	
Eland	0.6	-	-	-	1.5	-	-	-	0.7	-	-	-	
Kudu	0.4	-	-	-	0.5	-	-	-	0.1	-	-	-	
Oribi	-	-	-	-	-	-	-	-	-	-	-	-	
Reedbuck	0.3	-	-	-	1.2	-	-	-	0.04*	-	-	-	
Sable	-	-	-	-	-	-	-	-	-	-	-	-	0.4*

$\bar{D}$ = A density was computed for each of 8 replicate transects for each season (7 replicates for late dry season). $\bar{D}$ is an arithmetic average of the 8 (or 7) replicate D's for each season.

D = A density computed combining all data on a species during a particular season. This was done when date were not sufficient for a computation from less aggregate data.

D_g = Density over grassland portions only.
D_s = Density over scrub portions only.
D_w = Density over woodland portions only.
$\bar{D}_c$ = This density was calculated because insufficient data were available to compute D from less aggregate data. It combines the data gathered during all seasons.

* = These densities were calculated from less than 20 group sightings.

x = Data on duiker sighting distances were not recorded during the late dry season so no calculations were possible.

species is included for information only, with no confidence that they reflect reality.[1]

An examination of these data show that for nearly every species with adequate sightings, the grassland formations supported higher densities of animals than did the other vegetation forms. This is particularly true during the wet season. It also is true for the species most reported as having been absent in the vicinity of villages formerly occupied in the game reserve. (Referring to Table Four this would include waterbuck, impala, wildebeest and zebra.) Equally interesting is the fact that many of the species which were so rarely encountered that densities could not be figured were the very species reportedly present in every location in the past. (From Table Four these would include Sable, Kudu, Eland.)

It was the initial suggestion of this investigator that villages in the study area had occupied "critical areas" for the support of wildlife. By denying access to these areas, it was possible that villages suppressed the numbers of animals living in a locality. In order for this to be true, it must be shown that there was an inordinate concentration of animals in particular localities. From the data presented it can be seen that concentrations of some species occurred in the grasslands during the rainy season. It remains to be shown that the location of these concentrations is coincident with the particular locations chosen for settlement by humans.

---

[1] Bushbuck, kudu, sable, and oribi have insufficient data to be accurate. Bushbuck and reedbuck live in habitats which make their observation unlikely. Eland and buffalo occur in large herds which if included give extremely high results and if excluded give extremely low results. Duiker remain hidden until flushed, usually at a close distance. Therefore, the shape of their sighting frequency curve would not be a half-normal or a straight line. The 50 yard belts used to assign distances in this study are too wide to accurately reflect a true average sighting distance for this animal. Since this is the case, densities can not be calculated by the techniques used with any reasonable degree of confidence in the results.

Chapter IV

THE POTENTIAL FOR CONFLICT BETWEEN WILDLIFE AND PEOPLE

The Location of the Wildlife in Relation to the Location of the Villages

The previous discussion of the data from the wildlife census has demonstrated that five species showed particularly strong affinities to the grasslands during the rainy season. These were wildebeest, impala, warthog, zebra and elephant. Since it is the grassland habitat which is most restricted areally (present only in river valleys), it is the animals which favor grasslands that are potentially most disturbed by the strategic location of villages. It is in the study of the distributions of these animals that it is possible to locate "critical areas" for the maintenance of their respective populations. The data base for three of these species was large enough to permit its display in map form with considerable confidence in the reliability of the resultant pictures.[1]

The distribution along the transect line of wildebeest, impala, and zebra during the wet season (Figs. 24, 25, 26) shows remarkably little interspecific variation in their general locational preference. Over 80% of all of the individuals encountered were found in the three areas labeled as concentrations on the maps.[2] These areas are all river valley locations and

---

[1] The censusing problems with warthog during the rainy season were discussed earlier. The elephant numbers only totaled 341 during the rainy season so the inclusion of one sizable group sighting in any one mile made that mile seem quite important. The patterns, therefore, did not so much reflect a basic regularity as they did chance occurrences.

[2] The values plotted on the maps are adjusted to account for varying visibilities in the different miles as described in Matzke, 1976a. The adjusted percent of total numbers found within the three outlined areas were Wildebeest 84.6%, Impala 84.2%, and Zebra 80.6%. Their respective values before adjustment were 90.2%, 87%, and 82.5%.

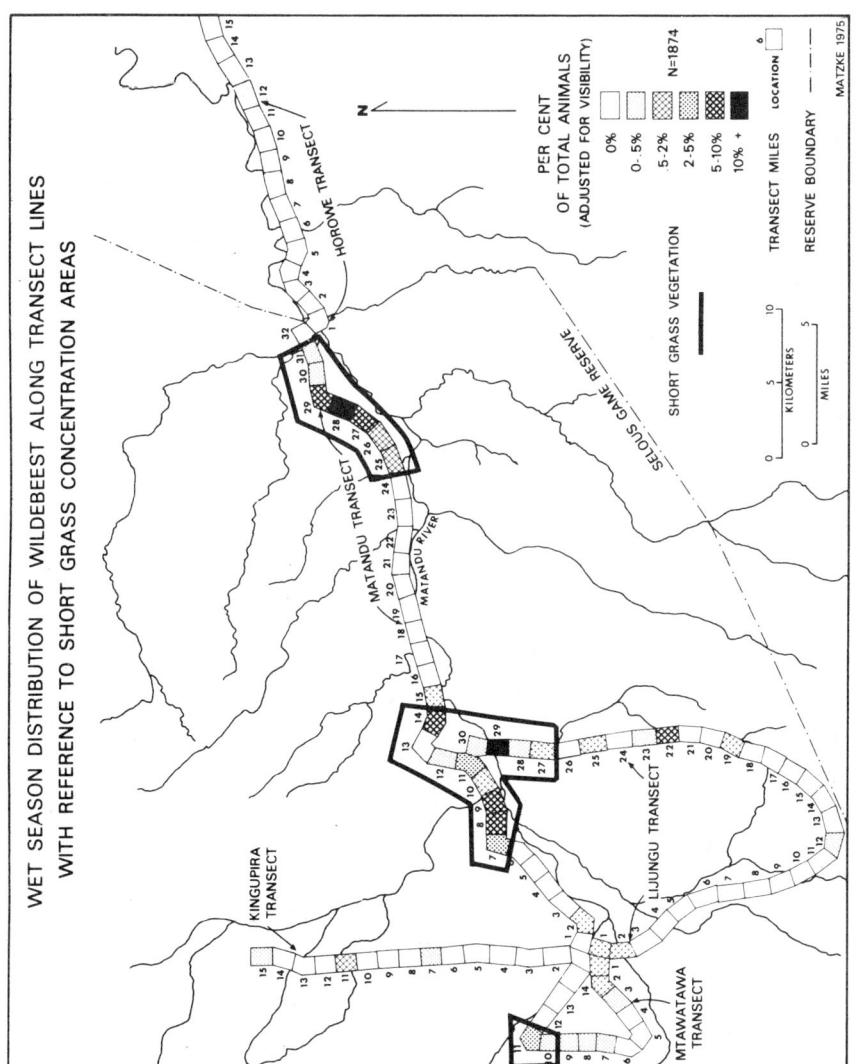

Figure 24

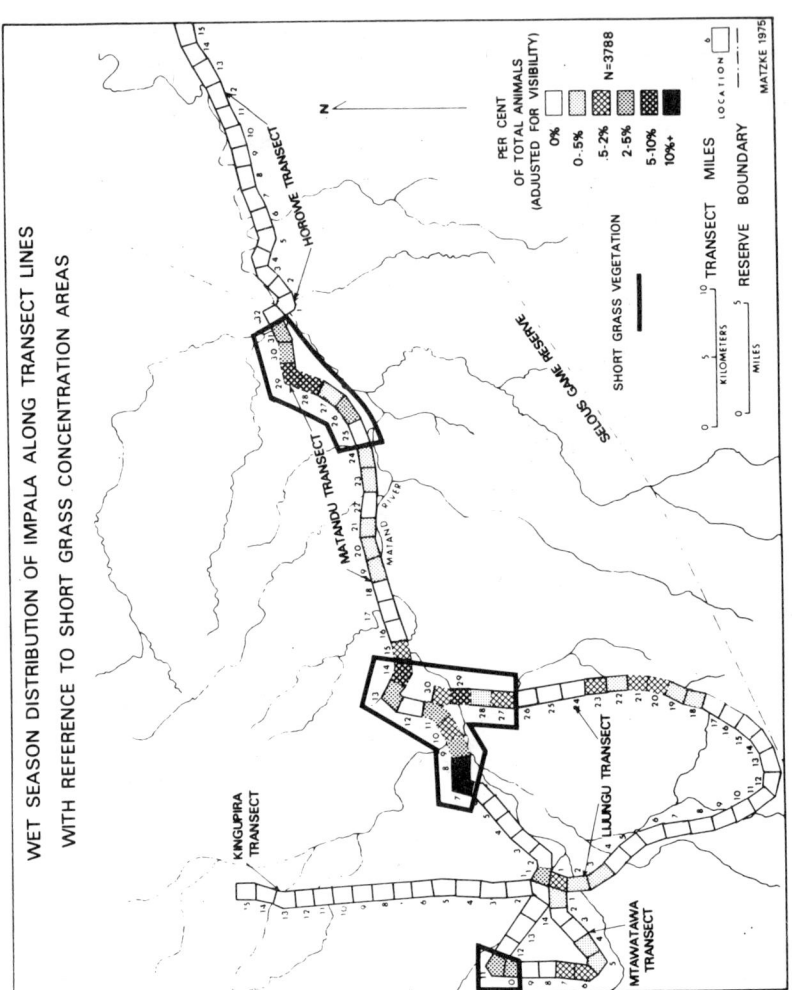

Figure 25

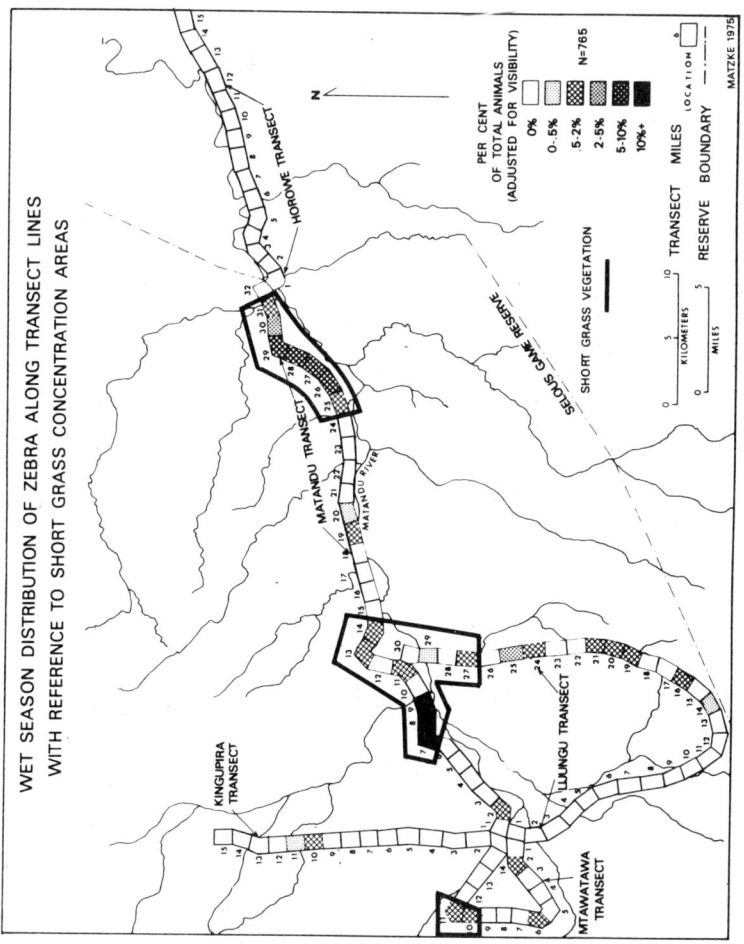

Figure 26

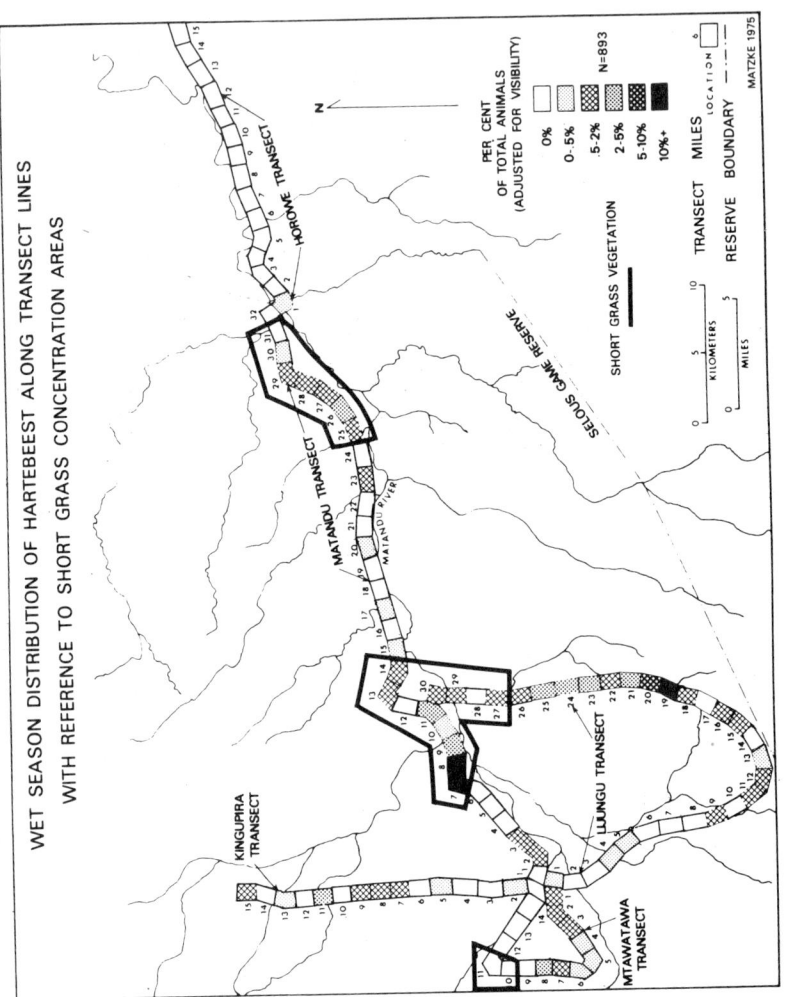

Figure 27

are either located on, or in juxtaposition to, the only sizable short grasslands along the transect cruise lines. Moreover, they are all within, or close to, areas formerly occupied by humans. Not all places formerly settled by humans were important for these grassland species,[1] but all important places were closely associated in space with human settlement.

The one woodland animal with sufficient sightings to facilitate mapping was hartebeest. The distribution of this animal along the transect routes showed a marked contrast with the distribution of the grassland species. Less than half of the adjusted total of individuals (45.8%) were found within the concentration areas demarcated for the species favoring grasslands. In marked contrast to the other species, woodlands with no history of human settlement proved to have a large proportion of the total hartebeest population.[2] The hartebeest population showed less spatial overlap with human settlements than did the grassland species including zebra, wildebeest and impala. (Fig. 27)

The spatial overlap between old settlement patterns and present wildlife distributions is illuminated in Figures 28-31. These figures superimpose an outline of the formerly settled locations along the transects[3] on the wet season distribution of

---

[1] For example, miles 12-14 on the Mtawatawa Transect followed "main street" of the old Muhinje Chini settlement. This hillside location was covered with second growth timber and was largely devoid of game.

[2] Of special note is the widespread distribution of hartebeest throughout the woodland localities. See for instance miles 4-26 on the Lijungu Transect and miles 2-9 on the Mtawatawa Transect which were never settled.

[3] On the basis of an examination of indicators in the field, air photographs, and interviews with former inhabitants, the outlines of the 20th century settlement pattern emerged. For the purposes of this paper, a mile was defined as settled if any part of it was within sight of locations which were known to have contained homesteads or fields. On this basis, 32 miles within the game reserve were classified as settled, 55 were not settled, and 5 miles were undetermined because of contradictory evidence.

four species. Data for all seasons and 12 species are given in Table Eight

The species can be placed into two groups on the basis of the data in Table Eight. The first group including hartebeest and duiker show no particular preference for formerly settled localities. The second group including elephant, impala, warthog, waterbuck, wildebeest and zebra show a strong preference for the settled miles during most of the year. This is as expected from the previous analysis of habitat preferences. The woodland species show no particular affinities to settlement sites, and the grassland species show a special preference for settlement sites which were located along river valleys where the grasslands occur. It is this second group which it is thought would be affected by the presence of settlement because their population distributions would have the most spatial overlap with human activity patterns.

Further support for this contention is found in Figure 32 which combines the information on species occurrence reported by former inhabitants of the game reserve with data on the present distribution of animals in the study area. It shows that the animals most reported absent by the residents are the ones which now have very few of their numbers in the unsettled locations. On the other hand, those species reported to be universally present in the past show stronger preferences for unsettled locations.

In order to understand this relationship, one should attempt to envision the consequences of reimposing human settlement in the study area. If the human occupation effectively denied settled areas to wildlife, then the consequences should

---

In addition, outside the game reserve 1 mile had abandoned settlement, 11 miles had active settlement, and 3 miles had no settlement history.
The lines drawn on the maps outline the transect miles which were defined as settled and not the entire area which might have been settled (see Figure 13 for this information).

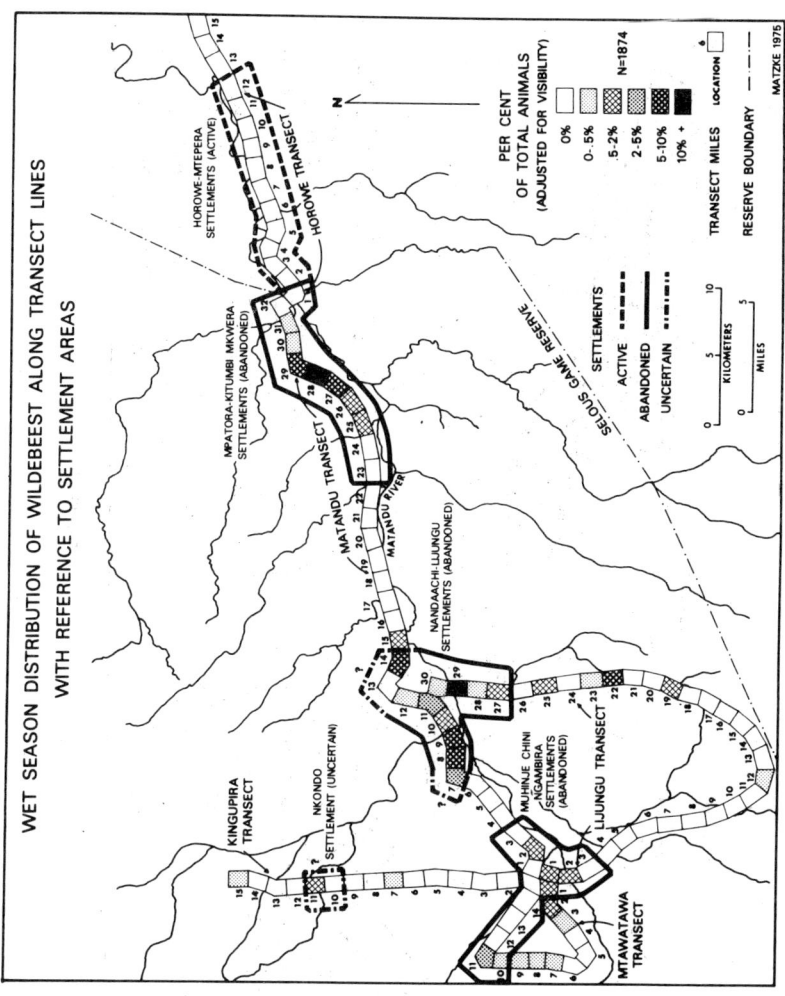

Figure 28

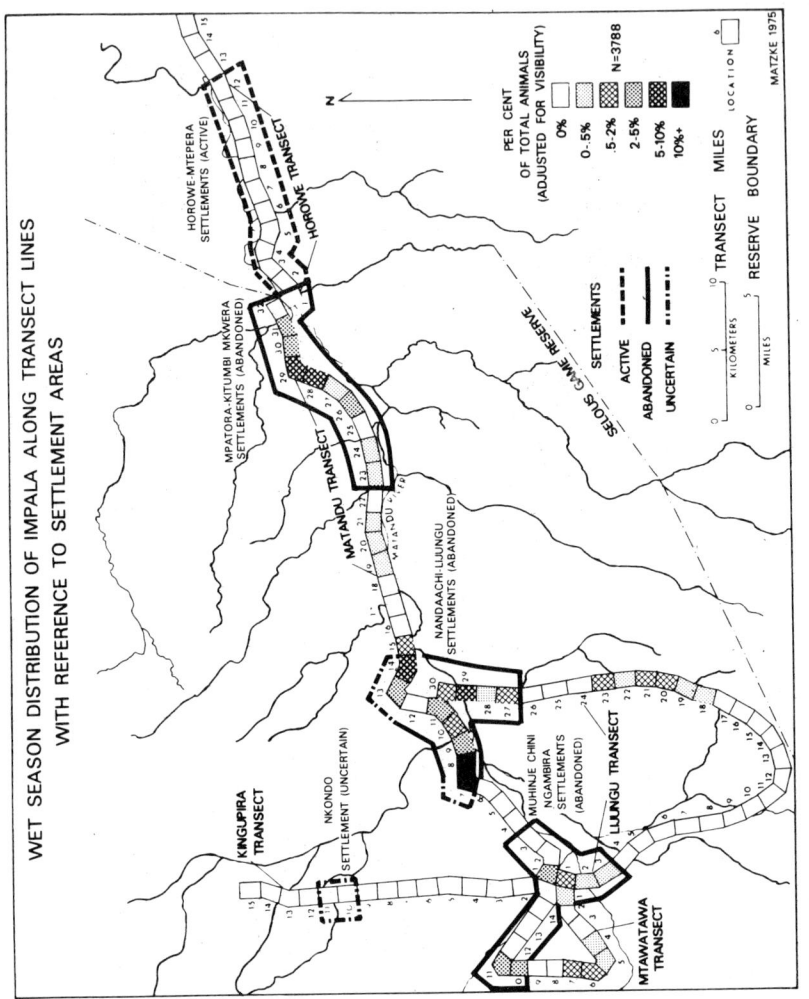

Figure 29

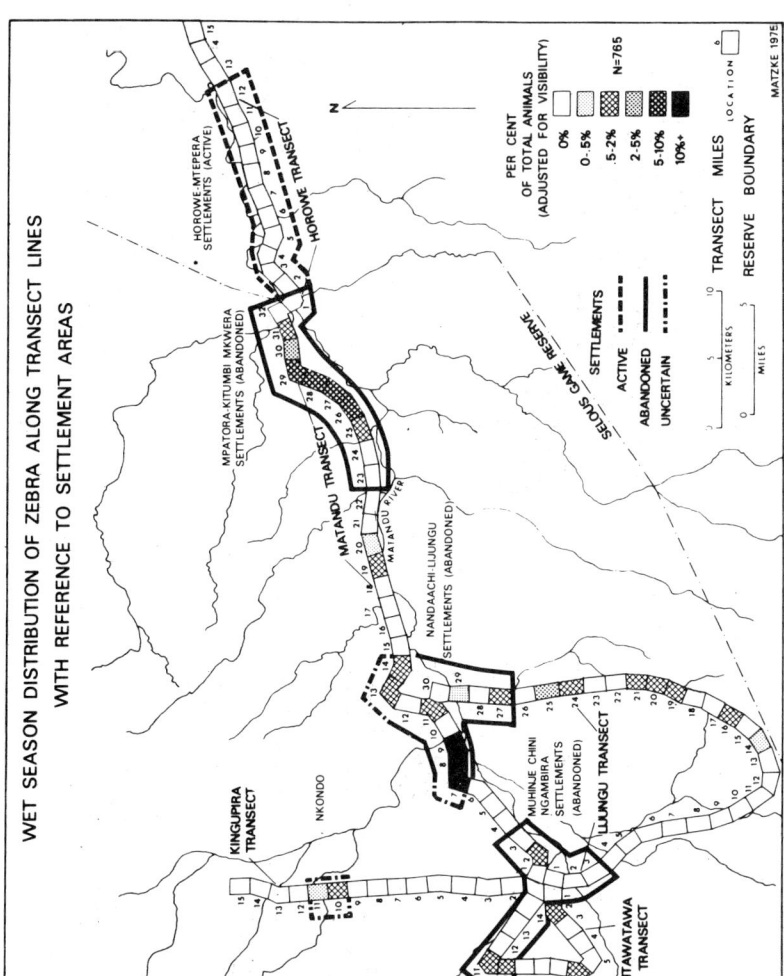

Figure 30

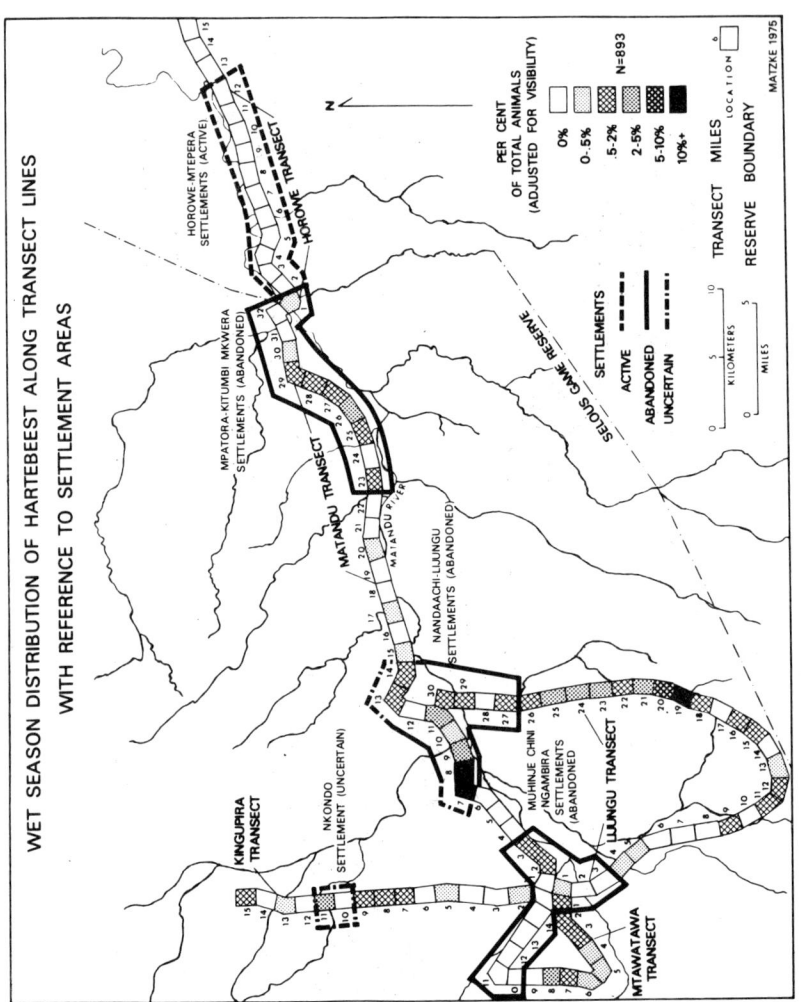

Figure 31

TABLE EIGHT

SEASONAL FREQUENCIES OF OCCURRENCE OF 12 SPECIES IN SETTLED VS. UNSETTLED TRANSECT MILES

SPECIES	Wet Season				Late Dry Season				Early Dry Season			
	N_a	$\%M_s$	$\%M_?$	$\%M_u$	N_a	$\%M_s$	$\%M_?$	$\%M_u$	N_a	$\%M_s$	$\%M_?$	$\%M_u$	N_s
Buffalo	496	5.2	0.2	94.6	787	42.7	1.0	56.3	2988	82.1	.1	17.2	43
Duiker	26	23.1	3.8	73.1	81	13.6	1.2	85.2	143	14.0	1.4	84.6	240
Eland	151	49.0	34.4	16.6	416	45.0	18.5	36.5	110	47.3	0.0	52.7	76
Elephant	257	72.8	8.2	19.0	270	30.7	0.4	68.9	339	53.7	5.3	41.0	274
Hartebeest	736	37.8	14.0	48.2	1244	25.8	9.8	64.4	1348	32.2	23.7	44.1	875
Impala	2539	63.7	26.0	10.3	1717	68.3	12.4	19.2	1890	67.1	13.3	19.6	755
Kudu	7	14.3	0.0	85.7	45	20.0	0.0	80.0	61	60.6	4.9	34.4	41
Reedbuck	6	33.3	16.7	50.0	203	27.6	13.3	59.1	53	32.1	0.0	67.9	128
Warthog	81	58.0	4.9	37.0	322	59.6	4.0	36.3	451	61.6	6.2	32.2	492
Waterbuck	117	47.0	0.0	53.0	325	52.6	30.5	16.9	421	45.4	0.7	53.9	218
Wildebeest	1117	79.0	9.8	11.3	565	57.3	7.4	35.2	870	76.6	9.6	13.8	323
Zebra	500	68.0	14.4	17.6	273	52.4	4.0	43.6	270	56.6	10.7	32.6	227

N_a = Adjusted total number of individuals. This is the number of individuals that would have been seen if the visibility along the transect miles was similar to that of the woodland areas (see Matzke, 1976a).

$\%M_s$ = Percentage observed in settled miles. This is the percentage of animals (adjusted for visibility) observed in the 32 transect miles (34.8% of total length) which were formerly settled.

$\%M_?$ = Percentage observed in undetermined miles. This is the percentage of animals (adjusted for visibility) observed in the 5 miles (5.4% of total length) for which the evidence of past settlement was contradictory. Usually the location was favorable for settlement, but informants could not agree if people actually ever occupied the sites.

N_s = The number of groups sighted during the entire census period. Generally, higher N_s values result in more reliable data calculations since the sample size of the number of places where animals were seen is increased.

$\%M_u$ = Percentage observed in unsettled miles. This is the percentage of animals (adjusted for visibility) observed in the 55 miles (59.8% of total length) which have never been settled during this century.

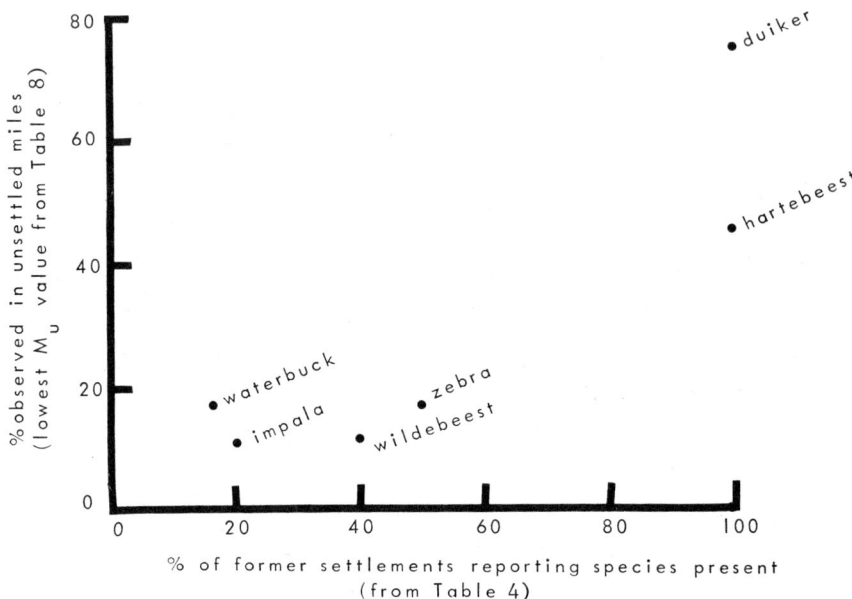

Figure 32 shows that the animals most often reported absent by former residents are the ones which now have very few of their numbers in the unsettled locations. Conversely, those species reported to be universally present in the past show stronger preferences for unsettled locations. It is suggested that settlement had much less of a negative effect on species preferring unsettled locations.

be much more severe for the impala population with only 10% of its individuals in unsettled areas than it would be for the duiker population with 73% of its population in unsettled areas. In the former case most of the population would be displaced, whereas in the latter case most of the population would remain undisturbed by the presence of humans.

With this relationship understood, it remains to be shown that the presence of human settlement actually denies wildlife access to settled areas. Under the conditions of very sparse human populations, this theoretical proposition is in need of evidence for its support.

The Case of Horowe Settlement as a Study in Human-Wildlife Conflict

It has been established that the locations within the game reserve formerly occupied by humans are especially important for the maintenance of current wildlife populations. The study included Horowe and Mtepera villages which were inhabited and strung out along the Matandu River outside the game reserve. The Horowe Transect passed through this very dispersed settlement and the records of animal sightings along this 15 mile route show a marked contrast to the data reported for abandoned settlement areas.

Figures 33-36 show the number of animal groups sighted during each of three seasons along the Matandu and Horowe transects. A total of 47 linear miles are represented in each of these figures. Miles 2-15 are outside the game reserve and had active settlement over part of their length.[1] It is clear that there was an absence of game in the vicinity of active settlement during all three seasons of the study year.[2] As

---

[1] In October of 1973, the number of homesteads recorded within sight of the transect were as follows:

Mile	1	2	3	4	5	6	7	8	9	10	11	12	13	14	15
# of houses	0	20	13	14	21	9	12	5	1	10	24	8	0	0	0

Miles with less than 12 homesteads were predominately bush, while miles with 20 or more had contiguous fields for a width of several hundred yards along nearly the entire length.

[2] Marks (personal communication) has suggested that this could be the result of a behavioral shift on the part of the animals. They retire from the settled areas during periods of human activity (daylight hours) and are therefore not recorded by the censusing technique. Attempts were made to assess this by examination of spoor along the transect and by censusing at both dawn and dusk. There was no evidence that the night time density in the settled areas was substantially different from that encountered during the daytime. It is recognized that many animals are more mobile nocturnally and crop damage is more likely to

Figure 33 Average Number of Sightings Per Mile Along the
           Matandu River (All Animals   Late Dry Season)

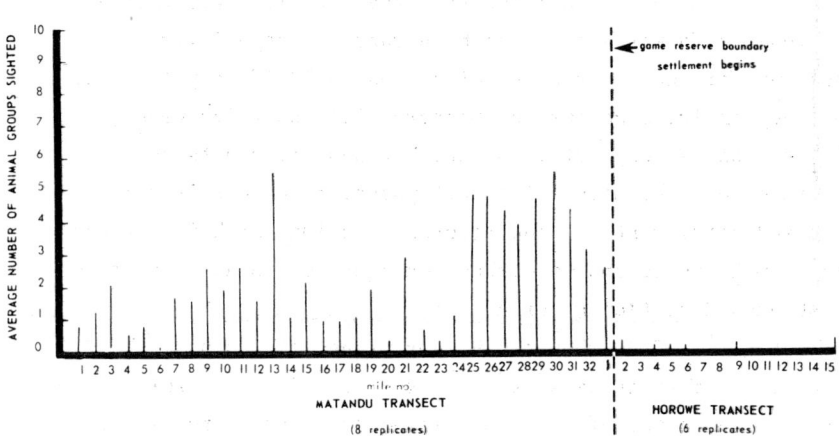

Figure 34 Average Number of Sightings Per Mile Along the
           Matandu River (All Animals   Early Dry Season)

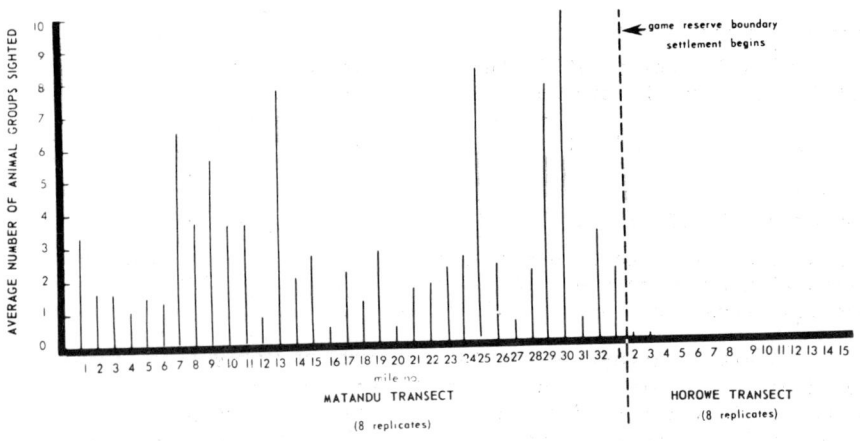

occur at night when there is the least human activity. It also
is true that it takes only an occasional visit from large mammals to do
substantial crop damage.

Figure 35 Average Number of Sightings Per Mile Along the
          Matandu River (All Animals   Wet Season)

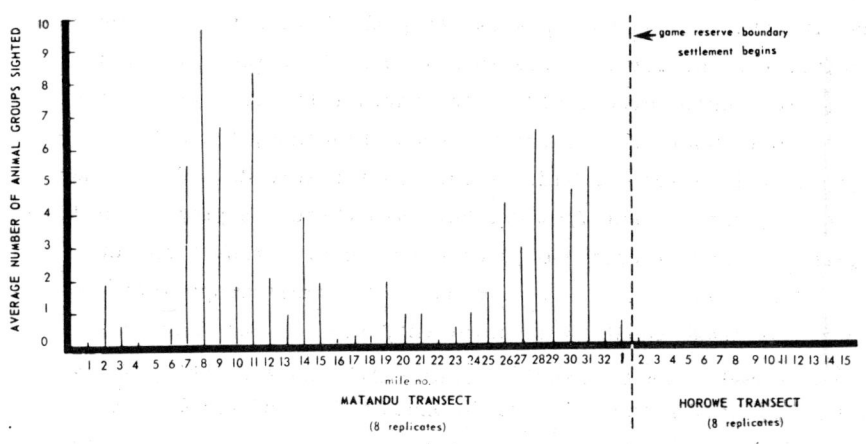

Figure 36 Average Number of Sightings Per Mile Along the
          Matandu River (All Animals   November 29, 1974)

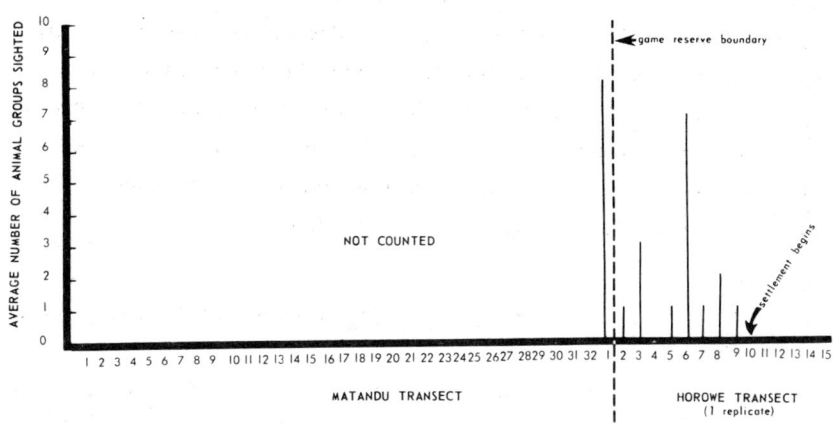

soon as the count reached the edge of the game reserve (which coincided with the start of settlement activity such as fields and houses), large mammals were virtually non-existent. This was true even though many places along the Horowe transect were uncultivated and certain locations were up to three miles from the nearest cultivated fields. In contrast to areas within the game reserve where settlement has been abandoned, the active settlement locations outside of the reserve were devoid of game. During the entire year from October 1973 through September 1974, a total of 22 replicate counts were made over Horowe transect miles 2-15. In all of that time only 10 animal groups were seen.[1] As these counts were being completed on September 29, 1975, the entire human population of Horowe Village was removed by the regional authorities to "planned villages" which were located some distance away.[2] In one move, the boundary of active settlement was moved from mile 2 to mile 10 of the Horowe Transect.

The effect of the movement of the settled boundary is illustrated in Figure 36. Two months after the removal of the people, one pass along the transect was made with more animal group sightings (16) than had been recorded on 22 previous counts of miles 2-15.[3] During the interim since the previous count, no rains had fallen and the resource base was essentially unchanged. The critical difference seemed to be the absence of an active human community. Where an active human community remained (starting at mile 10), no game was in evidence.

---

[1] A total of 16 warthog, 4 impala, 1 hartebeest, and 1 duiker was recorded.

[2] The move to "planned villages" was a part of a large scheme undertaken throughout much of Tanzania. It represented a departure from previous practice in which people moved voluntarily to cooperative, or "Ujamaa Villages." In this case, people had no option but to move. Many stories detailing these moves were reported in the press (Penza, 1974a, b). The abuses of these moves have also been reported (Time, 1975; Viorst, 1975).

[3] The record for miles 2-15 includes 23 zebra, 10 warthog, 8 buffalo, 5 impala, 3 hartebeest, 2 waterbuck, and 1 jackal.

The Mechanisms of Human-Wildlife Conflict

It has been postulated in an earlier work that villages in situations similar to that of the study area will be surrounded by a zone of negative influence with regard to their desirability for large mammal populations (Matzke, 1971a). The evidence drawn from the census conducted through Horowe settlement offers support for this contention. Although the occasional animal was seen within the disturbance area of Horowe, only warthog were encountered repeatedly. Given the fact that the cruise line contained a substantial animal population only two months after the human inhabitants were removed, it is logical to assume that the previous absence of animals was not related to an inadequate resource base.

The general absence of large mammals in locations with sparse human settlement has been noted by others. Leslie Brown (1967) wrote:

> ...in what at first appears to be uninhabited woodland, narrow paths snake from farm to farm, and one searches in vain for wildlife that should be found. Not only is most of the available land wasted, but another valuable resource (large mammals) is eliminated in the process (p. 44).

The common wisdom of popular writers on the African wildlife scene most often attributes the diminution in wildlife numbers to either the direct decimation of animals through hunting, or the destruction of their habitat as a side effect of agricultural activities. With regard to the particular case of Horowe, it would be difficult to support either of these arguments as an adequate explanation of the observed events.

Hunting undoubtedly continued in the vicinity of Horowe throughout the period of study. All legal hunting was stopped just prior to the start of this study, but Game Division personnel attached to the regional administration periodically shot animals as part of their crop protection and meat provision programs. This program continued after the removal of the people from Horowe. Several residents of the settlement were active hunters by their own admission and by the accounts of Game Division staff who had arrested them for their activities. It is presumed that the short move to the east did not force a discontinuance of hunting activities upon these people, and it is known that the shooting program of the Game Division was continued in response to demand for meat in the newly created villages. In spite of these hunting activities, animals had reoccupied the abandoned settlement areas within a very short time.

In the initial formulation of the problem, it was suggested that hunting activities were an inadequate explanation for the low wildlife populations thought to have been present when the area was inhabited by humans. Other studies have shown that attempts to remove most species by saturation hunting were unsuccessful in other parts of Africa (Child et al., 1970; Wilson and Roth, 1967; Graham, 1967). Marks (1973) has concluded that with regard to the animals hunted by the Bisa people whom he studied "any notion that hunters are a serious mortality factor in the survival of these ungulate populations can be disregarded." (p. 126) Hunting undoubtedly is one important part of the disturbance created around a village, but is far from an adequate total explanation for the absence of game observed before the removal of humans.

Support for this contention is found in the work reported by Wilson (1966a). In a Zambian tsetse control operation where hunting pressure was consistently maintained, hartebeest populations held their own for 20 years. As soon as settlement was introduced in the area, however, there was a reduction in numbers in the vicinity of settlement with no corresponding decrease elsewhere. Elimination of hartebeest in Wilson's study area was achieved only after the construction of a fence to restrict game movement. Hunting alone was not sufficient to exterminate hartebeest, or keep them from moving into unsettled locations.

Habitat modification is also an inadequate explanation for the pattern observed during the study of Horowe village. While it is true that cultivation activities had left many locations bare of natural vegetation, it is also true that this situation had not altered before animals had reoccupied the Horowe site. One would expect that after the rains had arrived, there would be a period when spilled seed from harvesting would give rise to volunteer crops of sorghum offering an especially attractive forage. Since the rains had not arrived, this was not the case at the time of the census. The only crops left to provide an inducement to animals were the cashew trees planted around many of the homesteads. These had been thoroughly destroyed by the activities of elephants, although no elephants were observed during the census.

Much is often made of the importance of waterholes to African wildlife, especially in the dry season. Since water is a critical resource for the maintenance of most populations, it was first thought that the need for permanent water supplies would bring man and beast into continual conflict. The data give no support for this contention. During the late dry season when the supply of water is most critical, more animals were found in the woodland than at any other time (Figures 17-22). The woodland is the driest habitat type (except for thicket) within the study area. Likewise, the formerly settled miles (which presumably are close to permanent water supplies) were generally less attractive during the late dry season than at other times of the year. (see Table Eight) This finding is not surprising given the widespread distribution of seepages in the Selous. During the period of time for this study, water was not a resource that seriously constrained the spatial options for most species.

The specifics of the interactions between man and beast are difficult to assess. It would appear from the foregoing discussion that hunting, habitat modification, and monopolization of water resources are inadequate explanations of the general absence of game in the vicinity of active human settlement. Nevertheless, the sum total of human activity appears to have had a significant "disturbance effect" on the distribution of most species, at least during the daylight hours when the census was undertaken.

If it is accepted that there is a "disturbance effect" around active human settlement, it should be possible to examine the data for the present day situation and determine the probable consequences for both wildlife and humans of a reimposition of an active settlement pattern in the Matandu Valley.

The Human-Wildlife Interface with Different Animal Strategies for Survival

The resilience of natural ecosystems is thought to be enhanced by the diversity of their component parts. With regard to the large mammal component, the African ecosystems are probably more diverse than any found elsewhere in the world. This diversity incorporates a wide range of strategies for survival which are displayed by the various human and animal populations in Africa.

The changing political, economic, and environmental conditions brought on with the twentieth century necessitated a change in settlement strategy for the Ngindo people. Their descent into more concentrated settlements along the watercourses fundamentally altered their relationships with the large mammals in their environment. In light of the material presented, an assessment of the possible impacts of their new settlement situation can be constructed. Many of the data for this assessment are summarized in Table 9.

The study undertaken by the author has measured several parameters of the large mammal populations which have spatial dimensions. The first of these is the average herd size. In general the larger the herd size, the less dispersed the population. It is felt that the larger herd is not to a species' advantage where there is active human settlement. Rodgers (personal communication) has suggested that hunting in such situations creates much more disturbance than does the hunting of more solitary animals where the shooting of one does not necessarily affect the rest. This contention is supported by work on elephant populations which were shot as part of a research program in Tsavo National Park (see Geist and Walther, 1975). It was found that unless every individual of a herd was eliminated, shooting of one individual spread a contagious and disrupting fear through the wider population.

Herd size is also important because of the general rule that large herding units are much more common in grasslands than in forest (Wilson, 1975). Since the grasslands are limited in extent, and often associated with settlement sites, they are the localities which are especially susceptible to human disturbance if there is active settlement. The habitual disturbance is accented by the openness of the grassland vegetation form. In grasslands, sound and sight carry further so any particular human disturbance action presumably has a greater areal impact than would be the case in woodland. The greater areal extent of the disturbance encompasses a disproportionate total of a grassland species' numbers because this area is coincident with the places of highest densities of herd animals.

Support for this thesis can be found in Table 9. Five species (buffalo, wildebeest, impala, zebra, and waterbuck) which have large herd sizes had very few individuals in unsettled miles (Table 12, column 2) and in woodlands (column 8). They were all grazing animals which are currently common, but were reported to be present in only a few sites in the past (column 6). The species with the most concentrated distributions now occupy the localities which were formerly most disturbed by an active human presence.

Eland and sable are two species which agglomerate in herds larger than family units, but each exhibits an important difference from the herd animals mentioned above. Eland take

TABLE NINE

SUMMARY OF DATA ON NATURAL HISTORY AND LOCATIONAL PREFERENCE BY SPECIES

SPECIES	Average Herd Size[1]	Lowest % in unsettled miles[2]	Grazer[3]	Browser[4]	Combination Diet[5]	% Sites Present (formerly)[6]	Present Abundance[7]	Lowest % in Woodland[8]
Buffalo	107.2	17.2	x			12	Very Common	14
Wildebeest	11.8	11.3	x			40	Very Common	13
Impala	11.0	10.3			x(g)	20	Very Common	29
Eland	10.3	16.6			x(b)	100	Common	26
Zebra	6.3	16.6	x			50	Common	11
Sable	5.5	61.3*	x			100	Rare	61*
Waterbuck	5.1	16.9			x(g)	17	Common	17
Hartebeest	4.3	44.1	x			100	Very Common	57
Elephant	3.8	19.0	x			-	Common	32
Kudu	3.0	34.4		x		100	Infrequent	61
Reedbuck	2.5	50.0	x			75	Infrequent	16
Warthog	2.3	32.2	x			-	Very Common	26
Bushbuck	1.9	71.4*		x		100	Rare	
Oribi	1.5	74.0*	?			-	Rare	
Duiker	1.0	73.1		x		100	Common	83

[1] Average herd size is taken from Table Five.

[2] The lowest seasonal M_u value from Table Eight. Low values indicate the species has very few of its individuals in areas which were unsettled during at least one season of the year. Those marked with an asterisk (*) were computed for the total count because data were extremely few--no seasonal computation.

[3] Animals were classified as grazers when all studies reported in the literature showed their diet to be predominately grass.

[4] Animals were classified as browers when all studies reported in the literature showed their diet to be predominately browse.

[5] The combination diet classification was used when the literature showed important shifts in the diet of the species from season to season, or from place to place. (g) means grass usually is the most important component and (b) means usually browse is important.

[6],[7] These data are from Table Six.

[8] This represents the lowest % of total individuals ever found in the woodland habitat on a seasonal basis.

mostly browse (Wilson, 1969) so they are not confined only to places with suitable grazing;[1] they have the additional advantage of not requiring free water, but can live on moisture obtained from plant material (Petersen and Casebeer, 1971). Sable, though a grazer, is essentially a woodland animal and often was not found in grassland and settled miles. Child and Wilson (1964) observed that the species avoids expansive open spaces. This habit would serve the species well in settled locations and should minimize the entry of sable into the disturbance area of a valley bottom village.

All species with less than five as an average herd size were either solitary or found only in family groups. It is presumed that this is the optimal strategy for coexistence with human populations since a smaller percentage of the population would be vulnerable to settlement in any one particular place. Except for elephant, members of this group had a smaller proportion of their total population occupying formerly settled locations than did the animals with large herd sizes.

Kudu, bushbuck and duiker are woodland and forest browsers which have not been eliminated by hunting in tsetse control areas (Wilson, 1965, 1966a; Wilson and Child, 1964). Likewise, the Lichtenstein's hartebeest, a woodland grazing animal, was not eliminated by hunting in a tsetse control program (Wilson, 1966b). Since they arn't especially vulnerable to hunting in the miombo habitat, nor concentrated on old settlement locations, it is thought that active human settlement would have no more than a local effect on the population of these animals. Except for hartebeest, however, their densities are uniformly low in the study area even without active settlement.

Elephant and warthog are two species which show some preference for old settlement locations, but are not thought to

---

[1] Wilson (1969) reports eland avoided active settlement in his study area. The data from my study show a preference for old settlement sites, but the sample size is small.

be seriously affected by the presence of active settlement. Warthog was the only species which did not seem to show an avoidance of the active settlement around Horowe. Riney (1969) reports that thousands are shot and left to rot in some Muslim areas. Their presence is observed near many settlements in southern Tanzania. It would seem that their dispersed distribution, the taboo on their meat, and the high reproductive potential of the species ensures their survival even in settled areas.

Elephants have proved their resiliency by coexisting with settlement and moderate hunting pressure for centuries. In the Southern Province of Tanganyika, the game division killed as many as 2,700 elephants a year in cropping operations (Ionides, 1965). Many others were undoubtedly shot by both legal and illegal hunters. In the face of such heavy hunting pressure, the population of elephants has survived. It survives by taking advantage of sanctuaries offered by both nature and government, utilizing a wide range of habitats, learning quickly the dangers of daylight raids on crops protected by armed game scouts, and by its near invulnerability to any foe except a well armed man. As long as settlement leaves expansive hinterland untouched, it seems likely that the highly mobile elephant will coexist with human populations. Since settlement often locates in places especially attractive to elephants, it is to be expected that any aggressive crop protection program will have the localized affect of denying these places to elephants.

Oribi and reedbuck are two species which were confined to the drainage lines and their immediate environs. This makes them occur in predictable places, but only the oribi is thought to be vulnerable to hunting because of it. Its peculiar habit of standing and watching a pursuer makes it easy prey to a hunter. Within the study area it is rarely seen, and settlement with associated hunting might well prove very disadvantageous to this species. The reedbuck, living in somewhat similar locations, makes much better use of both long grass for cover, and its legs for flight. Although its range is restricted to drainage lines, it includes extensive sections which were never settled. Unless settlement took up all of the drainage lines with their long grasses, this species probably would survive with numbers reduced in the vicinity of settlements.

After having reviewed the distribution and abundance of large mammals in the study area, the history of the inhabitants, and the relevant literature, it is possible to suggest some of the consequences of human occupance for the large mammal populations. If conditions of settlement similar to those found before the removal of people were reimposed, I would expect the following to be the consequences for the various herbivores:[1]

1. Only localized change around settlements, and total populations not in any danger (expected change positive = +)

    warthog   kudu   bushbuck+   elephant   hippo
    duiker   sable   hartebeest bushpig+

2. The total population's survival probably not endangered, but there would be important negative impacts on total numbers with a notable absence from sites where they are now especially abundant.

    eland   impala   reedbuck
    buffalo   zebra

3. Population's survival uncertain with a drastic change in numbers expected.

    wildebeest
    waterbuck

4. Very vulnerable.

    oribi

The above judgments apply only to the study area under the relatively light densities of Ngindo settlement and in the

---

[1] Very little field data were gathered on carnivores. The side-striped jackal appeared to be common only near active settlement so it presumably benefits from the human presence. Leopard might benefit from an increase in bushpig populations, but it is likely that a decrease in the populations of the herd animals on the grasslands would be detrimental to the support of lion and wild dogs.

absence of an important commercial hunting component. If different settlement arrangements, human densities, and hunting behaviour prevailed, different consequences would be postulated.

The Human-Wildlife Interface with Different Human Strategies for Survival

The Ngindo people have apparently exhibited three basically different settlement patterns over the past century. Each is expected to have different consequences for the large mammals in their environment and for their own ability to produce crops free from the disruptive effects of continual crop raiding by mammal pests.

The initial pattern consisted of maximum dispersal with many individuals located in thickets a considerable distance from the main watercourses. This pattern was replaced by linear settlements which were scattered along the watercourses in an often non-contiguous fashion. Finally, as a result of government intervention, many people have been moved into truly nucleated settlement arrangements where streets have been laid out and people all live in one location. These settlement arrangements are schematically illustrated in Figure 37.

Mascarenhas (1971) in his review of agricultural vermin in Tanzania has pointed out that where population is dispersed, cultivation is at the mercy of wildlife. The Ngindo tell another story. They say that before the return of the elephant to their country, their fields could be left unattended in thicket clearings without fear of serious depredations wrought by animals. If this is true, there are two factors which might account for the situation. In the first place, the settlement locations were not associated with the concentrations of game which have been observed in the river valley locations. The only animals with woodland densities of over one and one-half per square mile during the growing season of the census period were hartebeest and impala. Second, the proximity of homestead and fields which was possible

108

SCHEMATIC OF NGINDO SETTLEMENT PATTERNS

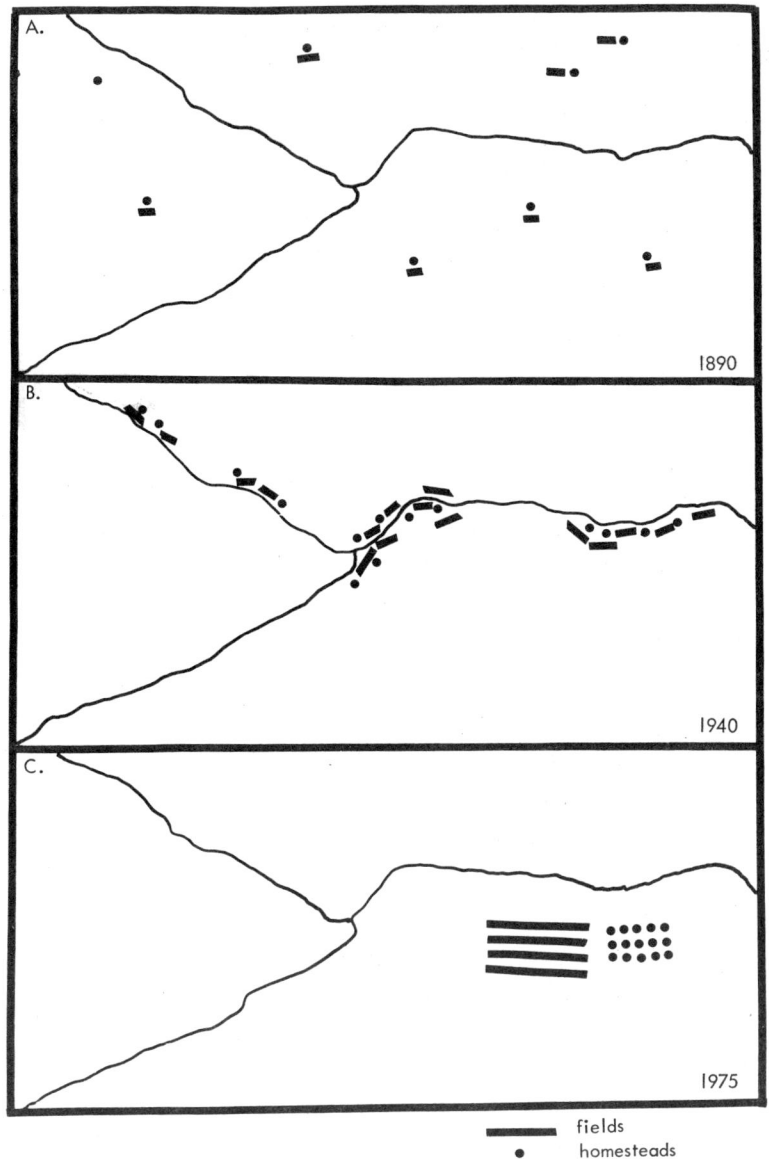

FIGURE 37

when settlement was dispersed in family units assured that some measure of observation of the fields continued even when no one was specifically guarding the crops. This situation changed, however, when elephants entered the scene and the people were denied crop protection services by the government. The settlement picture depicted in Fig. 37a was the least efficient pattern for the use of armed guards, and unarmed farmers in isolated settlements had a difficult time with elephants.

The linear settlement arrangement illustrated in Fig. 37b represents a period of time when the Ngindo people were most closely associated in space with the places now especially important to wildlife. Sandburg (1973) has pointed out that linear settlement arrangements produce a positive "interaction effect" with the addition of each new farmer decreasing the chance of vermin depredations. In areas with sufficient densities and provided with elephant shooting game scouts, the disturbance area along the watercourses might have acted to block animal access to locations which otherwise would be especially attractive to large mammals. The consequence would be a maximum impact on wildlife populations and a minimum amount of crop loss. This settlement arrangement prevailed during the time when Nicholson (1969) observed that game populations were at their lowest.

The nucleated settlements illustrated by Figure 37c have been imposed by the villagization program of the Tanzanian Government. It is unlikely that the patterns will long prevail since they do not conform to the cultural patterns of the people, or to the resource patterns of the landscape.

The dispersed linear settlement arrangements which prevailed in recent years allowed individuals maximum flexibility in the selection of field sites. People could select the most suitable location based on their assessment of the resources. House location could be adjusted, if necessary, to minimize house-field travel time.[1] In a place with a patchy distribution of

---

[1] Hirst (1970) found near Dar es Salaam that the maximum house to field distance was two miles.

soil types, the flexibility of the system was advantageous. If highly nucleated settlements prevail, it will mean that acreage planted on the better soils will decrease, or the travel time to the fields will increase substantially.

The Ngindo culture has incorporated a great deal of mobility within it. This mobility will be severely compromised by forced villagization. Since the plans as implemented are static, there is no place for the traditional nomadism of the Ngindo. If their previous experience with closer settlement is any guide, some modification is likely with people returning to a more dispersed linear settlement pattern if it is allowed by the political authorities.

The highly nucleated settlements remove much of the daily activity of a people from the vicinity of the fields and thus presumably decrease the "disturbance value" that keeps vermin at bay. This often is compensated for by assigning specific crop guarding duties to particular individuals and by the limited area in need of protection when fields are contiguous. In one case reported by Sandburg (1973), however, the efforts to combat vermin were inadequate to protect crops after people shifted from a linear to a nuclear settlement arrangement. The nucleated settlements are not necessarily a boon to crop production and protection, but the vast territories abandoned of human settlement are likely to see an increase in large mammal populations. The river valley locations are left free to be utilized by game animals.

*   *   *   *   *

The evidence examined in this monograph gives support to the contention that large mammal populations are strongly influenced by the pattern of human settlements. Within the study area, the presence of linear settlements along watercourses maximized the negative impacts on wildlife populations. The gregarious grassland species suffered the most because their wet season concentrations were in close proximity to valley bottom settlement sites. The disturbance effect of village activities apparently was sufficient to deny animal access to these critical resource areas. Their populations suffered accordingly. Animals with a preference for woodland habitats were less affected because they were not as dependent on village proximities for supportive resources.

The reorganization of settlements which is taking place in Tanzania will have consequences for the large mammal populations. The concentration of human settlement activities will likely prove advantageous to most animal populations in southern Tanzania since it will free up numerous critical resource areas for easy animal access. If wildlife numbers are to be maximized under any given human population density, linear settlements along rivers should be discouraged. Likewise, to avoid conflict resulting from wildlife harassment of settlements, compact housing and cropping schemes are preferable to scattered single family or clan group arrangements.

Settlement arrangements are not the only variable controlling animal populations. Their importance should not be minimized, however, since it appears that under certain settlement patterns wildlife would be virtually nonexistent even in the absence of human hunting activities. In addition, the settlement variable is one of the few that can actually be "managed" in Tanzania. Along with the control of hunting and possibly fire, it responds to the actions of government policy makers who can do nothing about variables controlled exclusively by nature. Because of its manageability, serious consideration of the wildlife/settlement interface is an appropriate endeavor for individuals concerned with minimizing the problems of agricultural vermin, and/or maximizing the benefits of the Tanzanian wildlife resource.

APPENDIX A

SPECIES LIST OF ALL UNGULATE AND LARGER CARNIVORE SPECIES ENCOUNTERED IN THE STUDY AREA[1]

UNGULATES

Common Name	Vernacular Name[2]	Scientific Name
Buffalo	Nyati (S)	Syncerus caffer (Sparrman)
Bushbuck	Mbawala (S)	Tragelaphus scriptus (Pallas)
Bushpig	Nguruwe (S)	Potamochoerus porcus (L.)
Duiker (Bush)	Ngorombwe	Sylvicapra grimmia (L.)
Duiker (Red)	Kidukwe (S)	Cephalophus natalensis (A. Smith)
Eland	Pofu, Mbunju (S)	Taurotragus oryx (Pallas)
Elephant	Tembo, Ndovu (S)	Loxodonta africana (Blumenbach)
Hartebeest (Lichtenstein's)	Kongoni (S)	Alcelaphus lichtensteini (Peters)
Hippopotamus	Kiboko (S)	Hippopotamus amphibius (L.)
Impala	Swala (S)	Aepyceros melampus (Lichtenstein)
Klipspringer	Mbuzi mawe (S)	Oreotragus oreotragus (Zimmermann)
Kudu (Greater	Tandala (S)	Tragelaphus strepsiceros (Pallas)
Oribi	Kimaru (S)	Ourebia ourebi (Zimmermann)
Reedbuck (Southern)	Tohe (S)	Redunca arundinum (Boddaert)
Rhinoceros (Black)	Kifaru (S)	Dicerous bicornis (L.)
Sable	Mbarapi (S)	Hippotragus niger (Harris)
Warthog	Ngiri (S)	Phacochoerus aethiopicus (Pallas)
Waterbuck (Common)	Kuro (S)	Kobus ellipsiprymnus (Ogilby)
Wildebeest	Nyumbu (S)	Connochaetes (Giorgon) Taurinus (Burchell)
Zebra (Burchell's)	Punda Milia (S)	Equus (Hipportrigis) Burchelli (Grey)

CARNIVORES

Common Name	Vernacular Name	Scientific Name
Hyaena (Spotted)	Fisi (S)	Crocuta crocuta (Erxleben)
Jackal (Side-stripped)	Mbweha (S)	Canis adjustus (Sundevall)
Leopard	Chui (S)	Panthera pardus (L.)
Lion	Simba (S)	Panthera leo (L.)
Wild Dog	Mbwa Mwitu (S)	Lycaon pictus (Timminck)
Civet (African)	Fungo (S)	Viverra civetta (Schreber)

---

[1] These include only those seen and positively identified by the author during this study period. It is possible that the following may also occur: suni Nesotragus moschatus Von Dueben, blue duiker Cephalophus (Philantomba) monticola (Thunberg), bohar reedbuck Redunca redunca (Pallas), cheetah Acinonyx jubatus (Schreber), black-backed jackal Canis mesomelas Schreber, and serval Felis Leptailurus serval (Schreber).

[2] If followed by (S) it is a Swahili name, otherwise it is of local origin, probably the Ngindo language.

APPENDIX B

DATA USED TO CLASSIFY SPECIES ACCORDING TO FREQUENCY OF ENCOUNTER[1]

Species	Animals seen per Transect mile	Assigned Category
Impala	3.91	Very common
Buffalo	2.18	Very common
Wildebeest	1.81	Very common
Kongoni	1.78	Very common
Zebra	.68	Common
Waterbuck	.53	Common
Eland	.39	Common
Reedbuck	.15	Infrequent
Duiker	.12	Infrequent
Kudu	.06	Rare
Sable	.02	Rare
Bushbuck	.01	Rare

Species	Sightings per transect mile	Assigned Category
Kongoni	.414	Very common
Impala	.357	Very common
Wildebeest	.153	Common
Duiker	.113	Common
Zebra	.108	Common
Waterbuck	.103	Common
Reedbuck	.060	Infrequent
Eland	.036	Infrequent
Buffalo	.020	Infrequent
Kudu	.019	Infrequent
Bushbuck	.003	Rare
Sable	.003	Rare

[1] These data are the result of a transformation of the data reported in Table 6 and were collected on 23 repetitions of transects totaling 92 miles in length. The total mileage 2111.4 miles was entirely within the game reserve. The species was given an assigned category used in Table 7 based on the highest ranking it obtained in either of the above rankings. If it obtained a lower ranking in sightings than it obtained in animals per mile, the lowest ranking was ignored.

BIBLIOGRAPHY

"African Update", 1977, *Africa Report*, March-April, Vol. 22, #2, p. 28

Anderson, B., F.A.O., 1960, "Soils of the Main Irrigable Areas," *The Rufiji Basin, Tanganyika*, Vol. VII, F.A.O., Rome.

Annual Reports of the Provincial Commissioners on the Native Administration for the Year 1937, Government Printers, Dar es Salaam, 1938.

Annual Reports of the Provincial Commissioners for the Year 1938, Government Printers, Dar es Salaam, 1939.

Atlas of Tanzania, 1967, Government of Tanzania, Surveys and Mapping Division.

Barongo, E. B. M., 1966, *Mkiki Mkiki Wa Siasa Tanganyika*, East African Literature Bureau, Dar es Salaam.

Baron von der Decken's Reisen in Ostafrika, 1871, vol. 1 and 2, His memoirs written by Dr. Otto Kersten.

Beardall, W., 1881, "Exploration of the Rufiji River under the Orders of the Sultan of Zanzibar," *Proceedings of the Royal Geographical Society*.

Bell, R. M., 1950, "The Maji-Maji Rebellion in the Liwale District," *Tanganyika Notes and Records*, January.

Brain, James Lewton, 1968, "Patterns of Continuity and Change in the Context of Planned Settlement in Tanzania," Unpublished Ph.D. dissertation, Department of Anthropology, Syracuse University.

Brown, Leslie, 1967, "The Destruction of Eden," *Audobon*, July/August, 1967, pp. 36-52.

Burton, Sir Richard, 1860, *The Lake Regions of Central Africa*, London: Longmans.

Buss, I. O., 1961, "Some Observations on Food Habits and Behavior of the African Elephant," *Journal of Wildlife Management*, 25(2): 131-148.

Capone, D. L., 1971, "Wildlife, Man and Competition for Land in Kenya: A Geographical Analysis," unpublished Ph.D. dissertation, Michigan State University.

Carneiro, Robert, 1956, "Slash and Burn Agriculture: A Closer Look at Its Implications for Settlement Patterns," in *Men and Cultures*, Selected Papers of the Fifth International Congress of Anthropological and Ethnological Sciences, September, Anthony Wallace, ed. pp. 229-234.

Child, Graham and Wilson, Vivian I., 1964, "Observations on Ecology and Behavior of Roan and Sable in Three Tsetse Control Areas," *Arnoldia*, (Rhodesia), Vol. 1, No. 16, 1964.

Child, G., P. Smith and W. Von Richter, 1970, "Tsetse Control Hunting as a Measure of Large Mammal Population Trends in the Okavango Delta, Botswana," *Mammalia*, No. 1, 1970, pp. 34-75.

Chisholm, Michael, 1968, *Rural Settlement and Land Use: An Essay on Location*, Hutchinson and Co., Ltd.: London.

Clyde, David F., 1962, *History of Medical Services of Tanganyika*, Dar es Salaam, Government Press.

Collyer, J. J., *The South Africans with General Smuts in German East Africa, 1916*, Government Printer, Pretoria.

Crosse-Upcot, A., 1956, "Social Structure of the Kingindo Speaking People," Thesis - Cape Town University.

Crosse-Upcott, A., 1958, "Ngindo Famine Subsistence," *Tanganyika Notes and Records*, June, pp. 1-20.

Crowe, J. H. V., 1918, *General Smut's Campaign in East Africa*, John Murray, London.

Culwick, A. T. and G. M. Culwick, 1935, *Ubena of the Rivers*, London: George Allen and Unwin, Ltd.

de Souza, Anthony R. and Philip W. Porter, 1974, *The Underdevelopment and Modernization of the Third World*, Resource Paper No. 28, Association of American Geographers.

Dorst, Jean and Pierre Dadelot, 1970, *A Field Guide to the Larger Mammals of Africa*, Houghton Mifflin Co., Boston.

Eberlie, R. F. 1960, "German Achievement in East Africa," *Tanganyika Notes and Records*, September, pp. 181-214.

F.A.O., 1961a, "Wildlife Conservation and Management," *Unasylva*, vol. 15, pp. 1-21.

F.A.O., 1961b, *The Rufiji Basin Tanganyika*, Expanded Technical Assistance Program, Rome, vol. 11, part 2, Map III.

Field, C. R., 1968, "A Comparative Study of the Food Habits of Some Wild Ungulates in the Queen Elizabeth National Park, Uganda," *Symp. Zool. Soc. London*, 21: 135-151.

Gardner, Brian, *German East*, London: Cassell.

Geist, V. and Walther, F., eds., 1974, *The Behaviour of Ungulates and Its Relation to Management*, International Union for Conversation of Nature and Natural Resources, Morges, Switzerland.

Gillman, C., 1936, "A Synopsis of the Geography of Tanganyika Territory," *Tanganyika Notes and Records*, March, pp. 5-13.

Glover, P. E., 1968, "The Role of Fire and Other Influences on the Savannah Habitat, with Suggestions for Further Research," *East Africa Wildlife Journal*, 6, pp. 131-137.

Gower, R. H., 1958, "Ukutu in the Nineteenth Century," *Tanganyika Notes and Records*, December, pp. 206-215.

Graham, P., 1967, "An Analysis of the Numbers of Game and Other Large Mammals Killed in Tsetse Fly Control Operations in Northern Bechuanaland 1942-1963," *Mammalia*, 31(2), 186-204.

Grey, Sir John, 1948, "A Journey by Land from Tete to Kilwa in 1616," *Tanganyika Notes and Records*, June, pp. 37-47.

Gwassa, G. C. K., and John Lliffe, 1967, Eds. *Records of the Maji Maji Rising*, East African Publishing House.

Hallet, Robin, 1970, Africa to 1875, Ann Arbor: University of Michigan Press.

Hibben, F. C. 1967, "Early Man in Southern Tanzania," *Archaeology*, Vol. XX, No. 4, pp. 247-253.

Hirst, M. A., 1970, "Rural Settlement and Land Use: A Note on Tanzania," *Professional Geography*, Vol. XXII, Number 5, September, p. 259.

Ionides, C. J. P., 1965, *Mambas and Man-Eaters, A Hunter's Story*, Holt, Rinehart and Winston, New York.

Jaghundbuch fur Deutsch-Ostafrika (1912), Deutsch-Ostafrikanische Zeitung, P.S.M.

Kiley-Worthington, M. (1965), "The Waterbuck (*Kobus defassa* Ruppell, 1835 and *K. ellipsiprimnus* Ogilby, 1833) in East African: Spatial Distribution," *Mammalia*, 29: 177-204.

Kimambo, I.N. and A. J. Temu, 1969, *A History of Tanzania* Northwestern University Press.

Kjekshus, Helge, 1977, *Ecology, Control and Economic Development in East African History,* London-Heinemann.

Knight, C. Gregory and James L. Newman, 1976, *Contemporary Africa: Geography and Change*, Prentice-Hall.

Lamden, S. C., 1963, "Some Aspects of Porterage in East Africa," *Tanganyika Notes and Records*, September, pp. 155-164.

Lambrecht, F. L., 1966, "Some Principles of Tsetse Control and Land-Use Emphasis on Wildlife Husbandry," Vol. 4, August, East Africa Wildlife Journal.

Langlands, B. W., 1967, "Burning in Eastern Africa," East African Geographical Review, No. 5, April 1967, pp. 21-37.

Lettow-Vorbeck, Paul Emil von, 1957, East African Campaigns, New York, Speller.

Leuthold, Walter, 1972, "Home Range, Movements and Food of a Buffalo Herd in Tsavo National Park," East African Wildlife Journal Vol. 10, pp. 237-243.

Lieder, G., 1894, "Beobachtungen auf der Ubena-Nyassa-Expedition 11 Nov. 1893 bis 30 March 1894", Mitt. dtsch. Schutzgeb, Bd. VII, pp. 271-277.

Lind, E. M. and Morrison, M.E.S., 1974, East African Vegetation, Longman, London.

Marks, Stuart A., 1973, "Prey Selection and Annual Harvesy of Game in a Rural Zambian Community," East African Wildlife Journal, vol. 11, pp. 113-128.

Mascarenhas, Adalfo, 1971, "Agricultural Vermin in Tanzania," pp. 257-267, Studies in E. A. Geography, S. H. Ominde, Berkeley.

Matzke, Gordon E., 1972, "Settlement Reorganization for the Production of African Wildlife in Miombo Forest Lands: A Spatial Analysis," Rocky Mountain Social Science Journal, October.

Matzke, Gordon E., 1971a, Settlement Reorganization for the Production of African Wildlife in Miombo Forest Lands: A Spatial Analysis, Master's Thesis, Oklahoma State University, 1971.

Matzke, Gordon E., 1971b, "African Wildlife vs. People, Politics and Plans," Proceedings, Oklahoma Academy of Science, 1971a.

Matzke, Gordon E., "A Historical Account of the Dynamics of Human Settlement in the Selous Game Reserve, 1850-1930", unpublished manuscript.

Matzke, Gordon E., 1976a, "Line Census Techniques: An Application in Biogeography", Discussion Paper Series, No. 11, Dept. of Geography, Syracuse University, January.

Matzke, Gordon E., 1976b, "An Illustrated History of the Selous Game Reserve",Tanzania Notes and Records, Vols. 79 and 80, December, 1976.

Matzke, Gordon E., 1975, Large Mammals, Small Settlements, and Big Problems: A Study of Overlapping Space Preferences in Southern Tanzania, unpublished Ph.D. dissertation, Department of Geography, Syracuse University.

Moyse-Bartlett, H., 1956, *The King's African Rifles*, Aldershot, Gale and Bolden.

Newman, J. L., 1969, "A Sandawe Settlement Geography," *E. African Geographical Review*, No. 7, April, pp. 15-24.

Nicholson, Brian D., 1969, "The Selous Game Reserve," (unpublished mineograph copy of a speech to the Second Annual Meeting of Game Conservation International, San Antonio, Texas), May, 1969.

Oberlander, R., 1903, *Eine Jagdfahrt nach Ostafrika: Mit dem tagebuch eines Elefantenjagers*, Berlin, pp. 406.

Otnes, J., F.A.O., 1961, *The Rufiji Basin Tanganyika*, Vol. II Part 1, "Hydrology and Water Resources," F.A.O., Rome.

Penza, Juma, 1974a, "Nachingwea's Massive Village Plan," *Daily News*, (Tanzania), August 26, 1974.

Penza, Juma, 1974b, "Marching Towards a Better Life," *Daily News* (Tanzania), September 5.

Peterson, Briand, J. C. and R. L. Casebeer, 1971, "A Bibliography Relating to the Ecology and Energetics of East African Large Mammals," E. African Wildlife Journal, Vol. 9, August, pp. 1-24.

Pfeil, Count J., "Die Erforschung des Ulanga-Gebeites."

Porter, Phil, 1976, "Agricultural Development and Agricultural Vermin in Tanzania", unpublished paper presented to the annual meeting of the American Association for the Advancement of Science, Boston, Feb. 23.

Pratt, D. J., 1967, "A Note on the Overgrazing of Burned Grassland by Wildlife," *E. Afr. Wildlife Journal*, pp. 178-9, V. 5.

Rees, A. J., 1963, "Some Notes on Elephants and Their Feeding Habits," *Tanganyika Notes and Records*, September, pp. 205-208.

Richards, Charles, ed., 1960, *Burton and Lake Tanganyika*, East Agrican Literature Bureau, Nairobi.

Riney, Thane A., 1969, "Wildlife Quality and Quantity in South Africa - A Reaction," *Transactions 34th North American Wildlife and National Resources Conference*, pp. 304-306.

Rodgers, W. A., 1971a, "Succession and Dynamics," unpublished mimeograph manuscript.

Rodgers, W. A., 1969, "Annual Report of the Miombo Research Center," mimeograph.

Rodgers, W. A. and Ludanga, R. I., May, 1973. *The Vegetation of the Eastern Selous Game Reserve*, United Republic of Tanzania. Mimeographed.

Rushby, G. G., 1965, No More the Tusker, W. H. Allen, London.

Sandburg, Audun, 1973, "Ujamaa and Control of Environment," mimeographed paper presented at the East African Universities Social Science Conference in Dar es Salaam, December 18-22.

Schnee, Heinrich, 1919, Deutsch-Ostafrika in Weltkriege Berlag Quelle and Mener-Leipzig.

Sinclair, A., 1970, "Studies of the Ecology of the East African Buffalo," Ph.D. Thesis, Oxford University, Oxford.

Smith, C. S., "Explorations in the Zanzubar Dominions," Supplementary Papers of the Royal Geographical Society, Vol. II, Part I, pp. 99-125, London.

Soja, Edward, 1971, "The Political Organization of Space," Commission on College Geography, Resource Paper No. 8, Association of American Geographers.

Speke, John Henning, 1864, Journal of the Discovery of the Source of the Nile, New York: Harper and Brothers.

Spence, J., 1957, The Geology of Part of the Eastern Province of Tanganyika, The Government Printer, Dar es Salaam.

Spinage, C. A., 1973, "A Review of Ivory Exploitation and Elephant Population Trends in Africa," E. Afr. Wildlife Journal, Vol. 11. pp. 281-289.

Spooner, R. J. and R. N. Jenkins, 1966, The Development of the Lower Mgeta River Area of the United Republic of Tanzania. Land Resources Division, Directorate of Overseas Surveys, Tolworth, Surrey, England.

Sutherland, James, 1912, The Adventures of an Elephant Hunter, London: Macmillan and Co., Ltd.

Talbot, L., 1962, "Food Preferences of Some East African Wild Ungulates," East African Agriculture and Forestry Journal, 27(3): 131-138.

Thomson, Joseph, 1968, To the Central African Lakes and Back, Frank Cass and Co., Ltd., 1968.

Time, January 27, 1975, "Ujamaa's Bitter Harvest."

Vesey-Fitzgerald, D F. 1969, "Utilization of the Habitat by Buffalo in Lake Manyara National Park," E. Afr. Wildlife Journal, 7: 131-145.

Viorst, Milton, 1975, "Social Experiment in Tanzania," The New Republic, May 10, pp. 7-9.

Von Prince, J., Gegen Arabaer und Negern.

Wilson, Edward, 1975, "Sociobiology and Ecology of Hoofed Mammals," Science, Vol. 187.

Wilson, V., and Child G., 1964, "Notes on Bushbuck (Tragelaphus scriptus) from a Tsetse Fly Control Area in Northern Rhodesia," Puku, 2:118-128.

Wilson, Vivian J., 1965, "Observations on the Greater Kudu Tragelaphus strepsiceros Pallas from a Tsetse Comtrol Hunting Scheme in Northern Rhodesia," E. Afr. Wildlife Journal, Vol. 3, pp. 27-37.

Wilson, Vivian J., 1966a, "Observations on Lictenstein's Hartebeest, Alcelaphus lichtensteini, over a three year period, and their response to various tsetse control measures in Eastern Zambia." Arnoldia (Rhodesia),vol. 2, No. 15, Jan. 21.

Wilson, V. J. and Roth, H. H., 1967, "The Effects of Tsetse Control Operations on Common Duiker in Eastern Zambia." East African Wildlife Journal, pp. 53-64.

Wilson, Vivian J., 1969, "Eland, Taurotragus oryx, in Eastern Zambia," Arnoldia (Rhodesia), vol. 4, No. 12, Feb. 1.

Wilson, Vivian J., 1966b, "Notes on the Food and Feeding Habits of the Common Duiker, Sylvicapra grimmia in Eastern Zambia," Arnoldia (Rhodesia), January 20, No. 14, Vol. 2.

Selected Files of Tanzanian National Archives

Provincial Commissioners - Southern Province

File Number	Name of File
1/102	Concentration of Natives 1932-48
19/74	Sleeping Sickness in Eastern Province 1945
19/75	Closer Settlement in Mbunga and Likuyu Areas 1945-45
19/77	Sleeping Sickness Transport 1945-47
19/79	Sleeping Sickness Measures 1945-47
22/3 Vol. I	Vermin Marauding & Elephant Control 1926-33.
22/3 Vol. II	Vermin Marauding & Elephant Control 1942-51
22/4	Game Policy 1926-50
22/5 Vol. II	Tsetse Fly 1933-51
22/5 Vol. III	Tsetse Fly 1951-53
22/17	Killing of Game by Natives 1928-47

Provincial Commissioner Eastern Province

File Number	Name
61/104	Deserters from Sleeping Sickness Areas Mahenge
61/104/H/1/II	Deserters from Sleeping Sickness Areas Mahenge
61/309/I	Game Reserves
61/504/1	1945-46 Annual Report 1945
61/504/H/1/I	

Tanganyika Secretariat

3046/9	Annual Report of the Game Preservation Dept. 1925
11234	Game Reserves Vol. II
11234	Game Reserves Vol. III
19838	Game Reserves, Southern Province
26899 Vol. II	Selous Game Reserve
26899 Vol. III	Selous Game Reserve
31756	Matandu Game Reserve

District Office Mahenge

44/2/37	Wangindo

Useful Tape Recorded Interviews

Horowe Village

Mohamed Matule

Abdallah Gabunda

Mzee Kujogopa

Sefu Kujogopa

Abdallah Pamunda

Mzee Keusi, Sr.

Mzee Keusi, Jr.

Ngarambe Village

Saidi Mwechandi

Mohamed Ligogi

Mchigagi Mfaume

Ali Kichote